GRAND PRIX
DRIVER BY DRIVER

GRAND PRIX
DRIVER BY DRIVER

First published in the UK in 2013

© Demand Media Limited 2013

www.demand-media.co.uk

Printed and bound in Europe

ISBN 978-1-909217-27-0

CONTENTS

Introduction

Right: *Shanghai International Circuit, China*

The Pau Grand Prix in 1901 was the first race to be given the name that is now synonymous with motor-racing, but it wasn't in general use until the Automobile Club de France (ACF) adopted it five years later. In June 1906, the ACF organised an event for 32 starters over a 65-mile course near Le Mans, but only 11 cars were still running by lap 12.

It usually took around 15 minutes to change tyres on early racing cars but Michelin created detachable rims and cut the time down to two. Hungarian Ferenc Szisz won the race in his 90hp Renault.

The grand prix in Le Mans was so popular that it heralded the dawn of a new era in motorsport, but racing was still fiercely nationalistic and many countries had different rules. While most races were run over closed public roads rather than purpose-built tracks, by the early 1920s rules across Europe were being standardized so that cars of differing power and capacity could compete in separate formulae.

In 1924 several national motor clubs formed the Association Internationale des Automobile Clubs Reconnus (AIACR), of which the Commission Sportive Internationale (CSI) began regulating racing before the FIA. Formula One can therefore trace its roots to the European GP scene of the 1920s and 1930s. The idea for a top formula was suggested after the Second World War and the first non-championship races were held in 1946. A number of organizations then submitted possible rules for a World Championship but these were not agreed until 1947 and it still took another three years before the first official Formula One race was held at Silverstone. A separate championship for constructors was introduced in 1958.

The 1950s were dominated by teams run by road car manufacturers – Alfa Romeo, Ferrari, Mercedes-Benz and Maserati – all of which had competed before the Second World War, and the

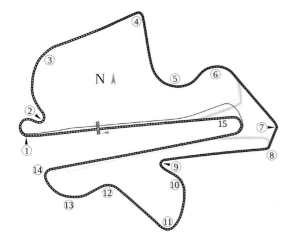

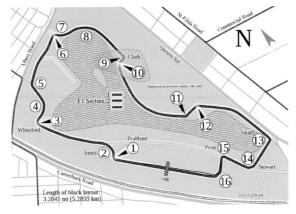

Left: *Albert Park Circuit, Melbourne, Australia*

Center Left: *Sepang International Circuit, Malaysia*

first few seasons were dominated by pre-war cars like the Alfa 158. They were front-engined, with narrow tyres and 1.5-litre supercharged or 4.5-litre naturally aspirated engines. The 1952 and 1953 World Championships, however, were run under Formula Two regulations because not enough teams could enter Formula One cars.

Italian Emilio Giuseppe Farina won the first championship with his distinctive straight-arm driving style honed from a career in hill-climbs. He graduated to circuit racing in a Maserati and then joined Tazio Nuvolari at Alfa Romeo. Three years later he won his last race at the German Grand Prix. In 1955, he started his final grand prix having taken painkillers following a starting-line crash which burned him badly. He retired after the Indianapolis 500 in 1956.

In 1954 the regulations changed again and cars were limited to 2.5 litres. Mercedes-Benz introduced the fuel injected and streamlined W196 and promptly won the drivers' championship. They would withdraw from all motorsport when Pierre Levegh's car left the track at Le Mans in 1955 and flew into the crowd, killing the driver and at least 80 spectators.

Alberto Ascari claimed back-to-back titles in 1952-53 but the decade was dominated by Juan Manuel Fangio. The Argentinean maestro won five championships, which stood as the record until Michael Schumacher won his sixth in 2003. Fangio is often called the greatest but he came to F1 at the comparatively old age of 37. He made his debut at the 1948 French Grand Prix but it was his only start that year. In 1949 he entered six GPs and won four. It was only when the championship itself was introduced that he cemented his reputation, and his 24 wins from only 52 starts is unlikely to be bettered. Fangio was kidnapped by Cuban rebels in 1958 but he was later released and became friends with his captors.

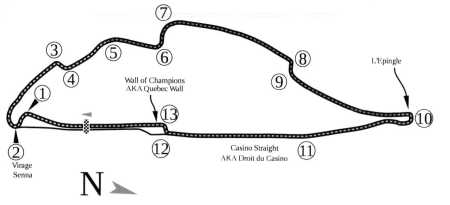

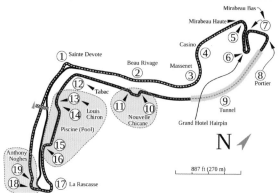

The end of the decade saw Briton Mike Hawthorn taking the title in 1958 and Australian Jack Brabham claiming the first of his three world crowns (1959-60 and 1966). Cooper re-introduced mid-engined cars (the first since Ferdinand Porsche's Auto Unions of the 1930s), which evolved from their Formula Three designs and Brabham proved their superiority. By 1961 all of the teams had switched to take advantage of better weight distribution and mechanical grip.

Colin Chapman came to the sport as a chassis designer but he went on to found Team Lotus, and his outstanding cars with their British racing green livery dominated for the next decade. Between them, Jim Clark, Jackie Stewart, John Surtees, Jack Brabham, Graham Hill and Denny Hulme ensured that British teams with Commonwealth drivers won 10 titles between 1962 and 1973. Both Graham Hill and Jim Clark won two each during the 1960s, while Jackie Stewart claimed the first of his three in 1969. Only Jochen

Rindt and Emerson Fittipaldi broke the monopoly.

Chapman introduced a car with an aluminium sheet monocoque chassis instead of the traditional space-frame in 1962 and it proved to be the biggest technological advance since the switch to mid-engined cars. In 1968, Lotus introduced sponsorship to F1 by painting Imperial Tobacco colours on their cars. Aerodynamic wings were then added to give them down-force. Jim Clark was perhaps the most complete driver of the decade. His career began in rallying and hill-climbs in his own Talbot Sunbeam but it was only when he teamed up with Colin Chapman that his career took off.

His early F1 career was marred by a serious incident when his Lotus collided with Von Trips's Ferrari at Monza. The Ferrari ploughed into the crowd and Von Trips was thrown from the car. He and 15 spectators were killed, prompting a major overhaul of safety. Clark won seven of the 10 Formula One races and took his

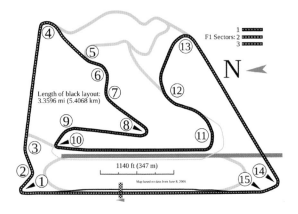

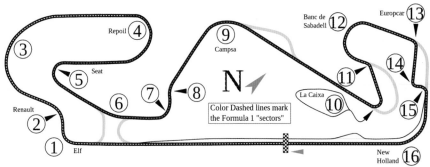

first drivers' championship with Lotus in 1963. Five years later, and with a record 25 victories to his name, Clark was killed when his Formula Two Lotus veered off the track – probably after a puncture or rear suspension failure – at Hockenheim and hit a tree.

Having made his debut at the 1958 Monaco GP (a race he would eventually win five times), Graham Hill enjoyed 18 years and 14 wins in F1. And all this from a man who paid for a few laps at Brands Hatch in a Cooper 500 Formula Three car. He then signed up with Lotus as a mechanic before persuading the team to let him drive the car. He later joined BRM and rewarded them with a championship victory in 1962. He rejoined Lotus after Clark's death and won his second title in 1968.

The 1970s saw drivers of five nationalities claiming the world title. Austrian Jochen Rindt won the first championship of the decade, albeit posthumously as he had been killed in

practice at Monza. Compatriot Niki Lauda took titles in 1975 and 1977, while Brazilian Emerson Fittipaldi also claimed two championships (1972 and 1974). Jackie Stewart also won two (1971 and 1973). James Hunt, American Mario Andretti and South African Jody Scheckter took one title each.

After Clark's death, Scot Jackie Stewart inherited the mantle of the best driver in F1. His career began with Tyrrell in Formula Three and he made his F1 debut at the South African Grand Prix in 1965. He retired in 1973 before what would have been his 100th race but, as he had already been crowned champion and he was concerned about safety, he sat the race out. The first of his record 27 wins came at the Italian Grand Prix in his debut season, the last in Germany eight years later.

Niki Lauda paid for a Formula Two drive with March before being promoted in 1972. His first year in F1 was unremarkable so he borrowed money

Above: *Circuit de Catalunya, Spain*

Center Left: *Bahrain International Circuit*

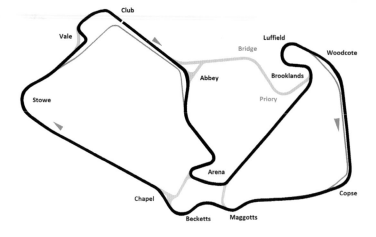

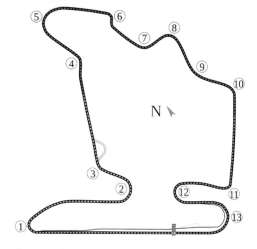

and bought his way into BRM the following year. On the recommendation of former team-mate Clay Regazzoni, Ferrari signed the precociously talented youngster and he duly delivered the 1975 world championship. He was on course for back-to-back titles but he had a serious accident at the Nürburgring and was twice given the last rites. Despite being horrifically burned, Lauda returned to the cockpit but couldn't prevent Hunt from taking the title. He was back to his best in 1977, however, and delivered the second of his three titles.

The decade was perhaps equally notable for the introduction of the ground-effect cars which used aerodynamic skirts to increase downforce and therefore cornering speeds. In an era of experimentation, Tyrell brought in a six-wheeled Formula One car and Brabham fitted theirs with fans to help them stick to the road. All of these innovations would eventually be banned or deemed unnecessary.

With three titles apiece, Nelson Piquet and Alain Prost dominated the world championship during the 1980s. Alan Jones, Keke Rosberg, Niki Lauda and future star Ayrton Senna claimed one title each. Piquet joined Formula One in 1978 but it wasn't until Brabham gave him a turbo engine in 1981 that he delivered his first title. His second came two years later but he then moved to Williams (in 1986) to partner great rival Nigel Mansell. He won his third championship after an epic season-long duel with the Englishman in 1987. He moved to Lotus the following season but couldn't recapture his early form and made several enemies with his outspoken remarks and general abrasiveness. (His son, Nelson Angelo Piquet, followed in his footsteps by signing for Renault F1 in 2008.)

Alain Prost joined the F1 circus at the Argentine Grand Prix in 1980. The meticulous Frenchman found intense

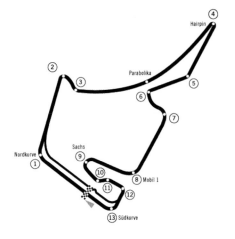

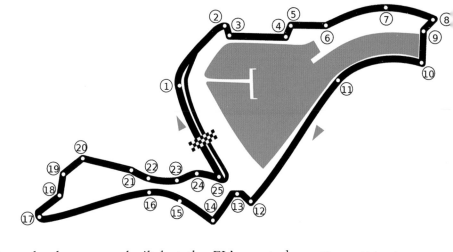

Above: *Valencia Street Circuit, Spain*

Center Left: *Hockenheimring, Germany*

rivals in the shape of Senna, Piquet and Mansell and the sport was much the richer for their on- and off-track tussles. His first win came at his home GP in 1981. He won the championship in 1985 and 1986 and secured a third after a collision with Senna at the 1989 Japanese Grand Prix. The following year the two men clashed again at Suzuka, with Senna the beneficiary. Prost took a sabbatical in 1992 but returned to claim his fourth title with Williams in 1993. He then retired as the most successful driver to date in terms of overall victories (51).

The Fédération Internationale du Sport Automobile (FISA) may have banned ground-effect aerodynamics in 1983 but turbocharged engines ensured that speeds were still dangerously high. In 1977, the Renaults were churning out around 700bhp (520kW) but by 1986 this had risen to over 1300bhp (970kW) in qualifying trim for the Italian Grand Prix. They were the most powerful open-wheel cars ever built but the FIA wanted to reduce power output and limited fuel tank capacity and boost pressures before banning turbocharged engines completely from 1989.

The decade also saw the introduction of electronic driver aids such as active suspension, semi-automatic gearboxes, launch control and stability control, but some of these innovations were criticized for taking the skill out of racing and many would eventually be banned.

The big four teams – McLaren, Williams, Renault (formerly Benetton) and Ferrari – won every world championship from 1984 to 2008. The technological advances made during the 1990s saw the cost of competing in Formula One skyrocketing and 28 teams pulled out of Formula One as a result. The days of competitive privateers like Eddie Jordan and Peter Sauber seem to be a thing of the past.

The 1990s were a troubled time

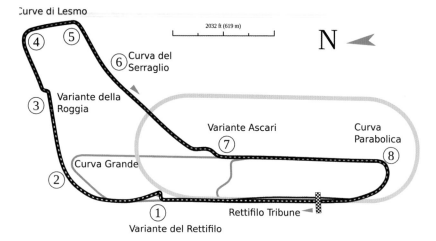

Curve di Lesmo
Curva del Serraglio
Variante della Roggia
Variante Ascari
Curva Grande
Curva Parabolica
Rettifilo Tribune
Variante del Rettifilo

2032 ft (619 m)

N

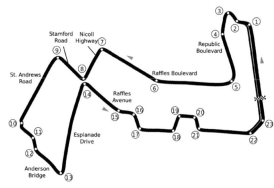

Stamford Road
Nicoll Highway
St. Andrews Road
Republic Boulevard
Raffles Boulevard
Raffles Avenue
Esplanade Drive
Anderson Bridge

Above:
*Autodromo
Nazionale Monza,
Italy*

Center Right:
*Marina Bay Circuit,
Singapore*

for the sport. Senna and Prost's rivalry dominated the first few years but the former's driving occasionally bordered on reckless and the two often came to verbal blows. Everything changed on one tragic weekend in San Marino in May 1994. Rubens Barrichello had a serious accident in practice and then Austrian Roland Ratzenberger was killed when his front wing failed and he crashed into the wall at full speed. There was then a serious accident at the start when a wheel bounced into the crowd and injured several spectators. But even worse was to come: Senna's car left the track at the high-speed Tamburello corner – probably after his modified steering column failed – and he too was killed when the car struck the unprotected retaining wall.

Michael Schumacher and Mika Häkkinen's rivalry dragged the sport from the depths of despair into the modern, safer era. But Schumacher

was never far from controversy, as his collisions with Damon Hill and Jacques Villeneuve attest. Schumacher and Ferrari dominated at the turn of the millennium and the team won an unprecedented five consecutive drivers' championships and six consecutive constructors' championships between 1999 and 2004. Schumacher's records include most GP wins (91), most wins in a season (13 from 18 races), and most drivers' championships (7). He always seemed to produce when it mattered, whether in qualifying or the race, and he is surely another candidate for the greatest driver honours. His streak ended in 2005 when Renault's Fernando Alonso became Formula One's youngest champion. Renault and Alonso won both titles again the following year and Schumacher retired after 16 years in Formula One, although he returned for another three largely unsuccessful seasons from 2010.

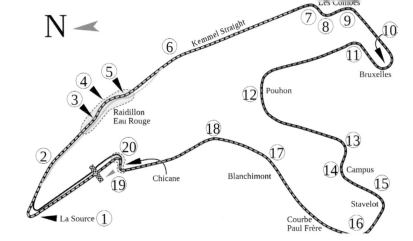

Alonso first raced in F1 with Minardi at the 2001 Australian Grand Prix but it wasn't until 2005 that he claimed the sport's greatest prize after wins in Bahrain, Australia, Monaco, Britain and Canada. He moved to McLaren in 2007, but rejoined Renault at the end of the year after falling out with team-mate Lewis Hamilton. Hamilton and Jenson Button claimed back-to-back titles for British drivers in 2008-09 but Sebastian Vettel won the next three for Red Bull and he remains the dominant force in Formula One.

The championship rules are frequently changed by the FIA to improve the on-track action and cut costs. Team orders, for example, were legal until 2002 but they were banned after several teams manipulated race results amid a storm of negative publicity (Ferrari at the 2002 Austrian Grand Prix is perhaps the most famous case). The qualifying format, the points system, technical regulations and tyre options have also been radically altered.

Grand Prix racing is still largely based in Europe, with most of the teams having factories and workshops in the UK, but the sport has now spread to the Far East, India and Malaysia, as well as back to the United States, where it is hoped the new circuit in Austin, Texas, will rekindle interest in the sport. Elsewhere, the races are massive international events attracting hundreds of thousands of fans with countless millions more watching on television. In 1999, new circuits were added in Bahrain, China, Malaysia and Turkey. By 2008, the World Championship had evolved so much that Singapore held the sport's first night race.

There are now 20 GPs in the season and, while most of the venues remain the same year on year, some countries boast more than one circuit. These circuits were used during the 2012 season:

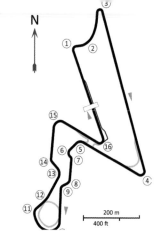

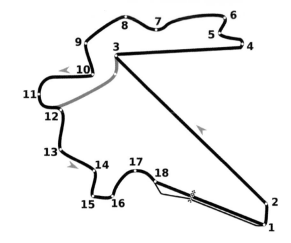

Australia (Melbourne)

With 58 challenging laps and a total distance of 307.57 kilometres, the Albert Park street circuit in eastern Australia traditionally opens the F1 season. Lewis Hamilton took pole in his McLaren but Jenson Button and Sebastian Vettel finished ahead of him in the race.

Malaysia (Kuala Lumpur)

The Sepang International Circuit is particularly challenging with its tropical heat, occasional storms and complex layout. 56 laps give a total race distance of 310.41 kilometres. Hamilton again took pole in 2012, but he slipped to third in a race that was won by Fernando Alonso.

China (Shanghai)

Round three of the 2012 F1 World Championship was held at the Shanghai

International Circuit. It consisted of 56 laps of 5.451 kilometres. Nico Rosberg took pole position and the race win, with the McLaren pairing of Jenson Button and Lewis Hamilton rounding out the top three.

Bahrain (Bahrain)

Work on the current 5.41-kilometre circuit began in 2002. It is also a popular venue for drag racing, F3, GT and the Australian V8 Supercar series. Sebastian Vettel secured the full house in 2012: pole position, fastest lap and the race win. Kimi Räikkönen and Romain Grosjean joined him on the podium.

Spain (Catalunya)

65 laps of the 4.66-kilometre Circuit de Catalunya just outside Barcelona gives a race distance of 302.449 kilometres. Pastor Maldonado took pole in a Williams

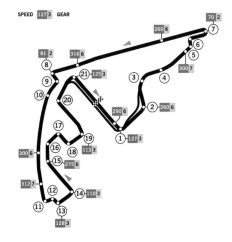

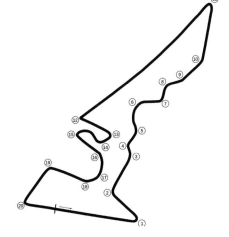

in 2012 and he held on for the race win ahead of Alonso and Räikkönen.

Monaco (Monte Carlo)

The 3.34-kilometre circuit in the tiny principality is particularly narrow and has a number of tight corners and steep climbs. This limits overtaking and keeps the speeds down. Mark Webber took pole and the race win in 2012, with Nico Rosberg and Fernando Alonso completing the top three.

Canada (Montreal)

The Canadian Grand Prix made it onto the calendar in 1967. The Circuit Gilles Villeneuve in Montreal is 4.36 kilometres long. Vettel took pole but Hamilton eventually won the 2012 race to become the seventh different winner that season. Romain Grosjean and Mexican Sergio Pérez followed him home.

Europe (Valencia)

Re-introduced during the mid-1980s, the European Grand Prix is a separate event in the Formula One calendar. The 5.42-kilometre Valencia Street Circuit saw Vettel take pole but home favourite Fernando Alonso the race win. Räikkönen and Michael Schumacher came second and third respectively.

Great Britain (Silverstone)

The circuit, which hosted the first F1 race back in 1950, has been redesigned recently and each lap is now 5.9 kilometres. Fernando Alonso took pole but could only manage second behind Mark Webber in the race itself. Vettel finished third.

Germany (Hockenheim)

The German Grand Prix at the

Hockenheimring consists of 67 laps and a total race distance of 306.46 kilometres. In 2012 Alonso started from pole and took the chequered flag ahead of Button and Räikkönen.

Hungary (Budapest)

The 11th round of the 2012 World Championship took place on the narrow, twisting and often dusty circuit just outside Budapest. The 70-lap race was won by Hamilton from pole, with Räikkönen and Grosjean also on the podium.

Belgium (Spa-Francorchamps)

With unpredictable weather and a beautiful layout through the Ardennes Forest, the 7-kilometre circuit is a favourite amongst drivers and fans. In 2012 Button drove a faultless race from pole to take the win. Vettel and Räikkönen rounded out the top three.

Italy (Monza)

The super-fast Monza Circuit was one of the inaugural Formula One championship races in 1950. Its 53 laps of 5.793 kilometres give a total race distance of 306.72 kilometres. Hamilton took pole and the win in 2012. Sergio Pérez and Fernando Alonso joined him on the podium.

Singapore (Singapore)

Each lap of the Marina Bay street circuit is 5.067 kilometres. Powerful overhead lighting is designed to replicate daylight but the drivers still practise and qualify at night to get used to driving in these conditions. Hamilton took pole in 2012 but didn't finish in the top three. Vettel, Button and Alonso took the podium finishes.

Japan (Suzuka)

The 5.8-kilometre track with its fast, sweeping turns, changes in elevation and great overtaking make it another favourite with drivers and fans. Vettel won from pole in 2012, with Felipe Massa and Kamui Kobayashi rounding out the top three.

Korea (Korea International Circuit)

This new 5.62-kilometre circuit was

the 16th venue during the 2012 World Championship. It has three long straights and an extended technical section. Mark Webber took pole but could only finish second behind team-mate Vettel. Alonso came in third.

India (Buddh International Circuit)

Round 17 on the F1 calendar was in India for the Airtel Grand Prix in Uttar Pradesh. The 308-kilometre race was won by Sebastian Vettel from pole, with Mark Webber and Fernando Alonso also climbing the podium.

Abu Dhabi (Yas Marina Circuit)

This technical 5.5-kilometre circuit has only been used four times by the F1 circus. Lewis Hamilton took pole in 2012 but Räikkönen, Alonso and Vettel finished in the top three.

United States (Circuit of the Americas)

The inaugural race in Austin, Texas, was the first grand prix to be held in

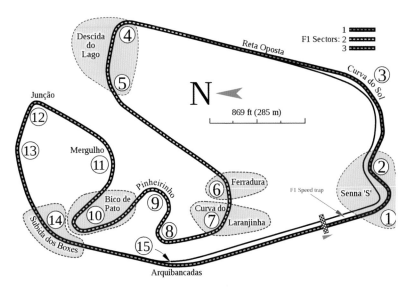

the US for five years. The track is 5.52 kilometres long and saw Sebastian Vettel on pole. Despite also setting the fastest lap, he could only finish second to Lewis Hamilton. Fernando Alonso joined them on the podium.

Brazil (Sao Paulo)

At 4.309 kilometres per lap, the circuit is one of the most exciting and challenging on the calendar. Turn one was renamed the 'Senna S' in memory of the Brazilian driver who died during the 1994 San Marino Grand Prix. Hamilton took pole and the fastest lap but team-mate Button took the race win in 2012. Alonso and Massa rounded out the top three.

Alboreto

Right: *Michele Alboreto*

Michele Alboreto began his career in 1976 in a Formula Monza car he designed himself. However, he didn't have much success until 1978 when he finished third in the Italian Formula Three series.

He signed for Minardi's Formula Two team in 1981 and made his Formula One debut later that year in a Tyrrell at San Marino. Alboreto stayed with Tyrrell until 1983 before moving to Ferrari. The following year he finished fourth in the championship, and two wins in 1985 saw him finish runner up in the drivers' standings, but he couldn't improve and returned to Tyrrell in 1989. Success proved elusive and, despite driving for several other teams, he retired from Formula One at the end of 1994.

Alboreto went on to win Le Mans in 1997 in a TWR-run Porsche. He was killed in 2001 while testing an Audi R8.

Name: Michele ALBORETO
Nationality: Italian
Born: 23rd December 1956
Died: 25th April 2001
Seasons: 1981–1994
Team/manufacturer(s): Tyrrell, Ferrari, Larrousse, Arrows, Minardi
Grand Prix: 215
Race wins: 5
Championship wins: 0

Alesi

Jean Alesi began his motorsport career as a rally driver but he graduated to single-seaters and won the 1988 French Formula Three championship and the 1989 International Formula 3000 series.

He finished fourth in his first Formula One outing at his home grand prix in 1989. After a successful 1990 season, Alesi's stock was on the rise and he signed for Ferrari. The Italians proved to be a poor choice, however, because the team was under-performing and he had little success in five years despite winning over the tifosi (passionate Ferrari fans).

Although a skilful driver, Alesi was dogged by bad luck and he only won one grand prix at Montreal in 1995. After retiring from Formula One at the end of 2001, he raced in the DTM German touring cars series.

Above: *Jean Alesi crosses the finish line in his Scuderia Ferrari, 1995*

Left: *Jean Alesi concentrates during qualifying for the Hungarian Grand Prix*

Name: Giovanni (Jean) ALESI
Nationality: French
Born: 11th June 1964
Seasons: 1989-2001
Team/manufacturer(s): Tyrrell, Ferrari, Benetton, Sauber, Prost, Jordan
Grand Prix: 202
Race wins: 1
Championship wins: 0

Alonso

In 2005, aged only 24, Fernando Alonso won the World Drivers' Championship, ending Schumacher's reign and becoming the youngest driver to take the title.

Alonso was inspired by his father's passion for kart racing. José Luis wanted his children to continue his hobby so he built his eight-year-old daughter a simple kart. She didn't take to the sport so three-year-old Fernando was given the machine instead.

Alonso was a natural and in 1988, at the age of seven, he won all eight races in the Pola de Laviana Championship and took the title. He went on to win the Spanish Kart Championship in 1994, 1996 and 1997, and he was the World Junior Karting Champion in 1996.

At the age of 18, Alonso won the Spanish Nissan Open Series, which guaranteed him a place in Formula 3000 the following season. He promptly won at Spa and was asked to drive for the Minardi Formula One team in 2001. Despite delivering several good performances, he failed to score any points in his first year.

Alonso signed up as Renault's test driver in 2002 and he was handed the race seat the following year. He repaid the faith by scoring points throughout the campaign, winning the Hungarian Grand Prix (becoming the youngest driver ever to win a Formula One race) and finishing the season in sixth place. Despite not winning a race in his next season, he drove consistently and finished in the points 12 times, securing fourth place in the championship in the process.

In 2005 Alonso finished third in the

first race of the season (in Australia), then won his next three grands prix, in Malaysia, Bahrain and Italy. He also won at Monaco, the Nürburgring, France, Germany and China. Consistent podium positions in between and a third place in Brazil secured him his first drivers' championship. At 24 years and 59 days, Alonso was 18 months younger than the previous youngest champion, Brazilian Emerson Fittipaldi.

By the end of the season, the young Spaniard had helped Renault to the constructors' championship for the first time. He secured a second championship the following year with seven irresistible victories and another seven second-place finishes.

Alonso moved to McLaren in 2007 and scored his first win in only his second race for the team. The season was marred by a bitter feud with team-mate Lewis Hamilton, however, and Alonso left for Renault having finished third in the championship (level on points with Hamilton and just one behind Kimi Räikkönen).

The 2008 campaign proved difficult and he only managed two wins towards the end of the season. He ended up fifth overall, a poor return for such a talented driver. The following season his car wasn't

competitive and he could only finish ninth with 26 points. A move to Ferrari for 2010 saw an upsurge in fortunes and he notched five wins, only losing out to Sebastian Vettel in the title race. In 2011 he only managed a single win at Silverstone, but 2012 was extremely hard-fought and he pushed Vettel all the way. Had he scored more points towards the end of the season he would surely have taken the title.

Above: *The Renault of Fernando Alonso leads at the first corner during the 2008 Singapore Grand Prix*

Name: Fernando ALONSO
Nationality: Spanish
Born: 29th July 1981
Seasons: 2001–
Team/manufacturer(s): Minardi, Renault, Ferrari
Grand Prix: 198
Race wins: 30
Championship wins: 2

Andretti

Mario Andretti is the only person to have won the Formula One World Championship, the Indianapolis 500 and the Daytona 500. The family name is as well-known in America as that of Moss, Mansell or Hill in the UK.

Born in Italy, Andretti's family emigrated to the USA and settled in Pennsylvania. He and his twin brother, Aldo, took to racing an old Hudson around dirt tracks, and Mario was soon competing in USAC sprint car and IndyCar racing. In 1965 he entered the Indianapolis 500 and came third, taking the Rookie of the Year award (he eventually won the event in 1969, the first of four titles).

Lotus team principal Colin Chapman noticed Andretti's talent and promised him a drive in one of his cars so, in 1968, Andretti entered his first grand prix at Watkins Glen. Driving a Lotus 49B, he took pole position but had to retire from the race due to mechanical problems.

Andretti raced sporadically in Formula One for the next few years, winning his first race with a Ferrari in 1971 before signing for Parnelli. However, because he was still racing in USAC events (travelling back and forth across the Atlantic on Concorde) he couldn't devote himself to Formula One until 1976. Now back with Lotus, he claimed the 1978 World Championship.

Sadly they were unable to repeat their success in 1979 and Andretti eventually moved to Alfa Romeo. Another poor season saw him return to Ferrari at the end of 1982, after which he retired from Formula One. He continued to drive Champ Cars, however, and competed at Le Mans until 2000. He was the first driver to win IndyCar races in four different decades, and remains the only driver to win a recognised motor race in five separate decades.

Name: Mario Gabriele ANDRETTI
Nationality: American
Born: 28th February 1940
Seasons: 1968-1972, 1974-1982
Team/manufacturer(s): Lotus, STP Corporation, Ferrari, Parnelli, Alfa Romeo, Williams
Grand Prix: 131
Race wins: 12
Championship wins: 1

Arnoux

René Arnoux was born in Grenoble, France, and his career started when he went to Italy to race karts. He graduated to the Volant Shell Championship and then Formula Renault, a series he won in 1973. Two years later he took the European Super Renault title before moving into Formula Two. In 1977, driving for Martini, he became champion.

When Martini moved into Formula One, Arnoux was chosen as a driver, although the cars were uncompetitive and he had limited success. He landed a dream move to Renault in 1979 and results improved to the point where he finished sixth in the 1980 championship.

His driving attracted the attention of Ferrari, a team he signed for after falling out with team-mate Alain Prost. His best year was 1983 when he won the Canadian, German and Dutch Grands Prix and took third place in the championship.

In 1989, after an unsuccessful move to Ligier, Arnoux retired to help manage a Formula 3000 team, although he did appear alongside Andrea de Cesaris and Nigel Mansell in 2006 in the short-lived GP Masters series.

Name: René Alexandre ARNOUX
Nationality: French
Born: 4th July 1948
Seasons: 1978-1989
Team/manufacturer(s): Martini, Surtees, Renault, Ferrari, Ligier
Grand Prix: 165
Race wins: 7
Championship wins: 0

Ascari, Alberto

Alberto Ascari was seven when father Antonio was killed at the French Grand Prix, but he wasn't put off a career in motorsport and developed into one of the great drivers of his era.

After racing motorcycles, Ascari's first taste of a road race was the 1940 Mille Miglia in a Ferrari. After the war he bought a 3CLT Maserati and won the 1948 San Remo Grand Prix. The following season he triumphed in the Swiss and European GPs.

He drove for Ferrari in the first Formula One season in 1950 and finished in fifth place overall after several notable victories. Despite not all the races counting towards the drivers' championship, he scored another six wins in 1951, 11 in 1952 and eight in 1953, the latter two years seeing him crowned world champion.

In 1952, Ascari became the only European driver to race in the Indy 500 and, although he failed to finish, it was the only grand prix he didn't win that season. He then moved to Lancia but failed to finish a single race. The 1955 season began in a similar vein, with Ascari retiring from the first two races, the second after a spectacular crash into Monaco's harbour after missing a chicane. Thankfully he managed to escape the sinking car.

A week later, Ascari took a friend's Ferrari onto the track Monza but, for reasons that have never been fully explained, the car skidded coming out of a bend and turned over. Ascari was thrown onto the track and died of his injuries.

Name: Alberto ASCARI
Nationality: Italian
Born: 13th July 1918
Died: 26th May 1955
Seasons: 1950–1955
Team/manufacturer(s): Ferrari, Maserati, Lancia
Grand Prix: 32
Race wins: 13
Championship wins: 2

Ascari, Antonio

It would be churlish to write a book about the great grand prix drivers without including some of the pre-Formula One giants, and Antonio Ascari was just that. He raced before the First World War but became a household name afterwards when he won several hill-climbs and notable races at Cremona in an Alfa Romeo.

Bad luck cost him early GP victories but he won in Italy, Europe and Spa, and he was leading the French Grand Prix when he slid wide on a wet corner and flipped the car. He died in remarkably similar circumstances to those that would claim his son 30 years later.

Above: *Antonio Ascari*

Left: *Enzo Ferrari congratulates Antonio Ascari after a race win*

Name: Antonio ASCARI
Nationality: Italian
Born: 15th September 1888
Died: 26th July 1925
Seasons: 1914-1925
Team/manufacturer(s): De Vecchi, Fiat, Alfa Romeo
Race wins: 3
Championship wins: 0

Barrichello

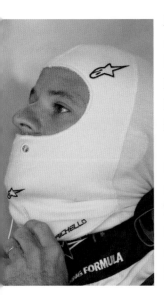

As a youngster, Rubens Barrichello won five karting championships in Brazil. He moved to Europe in 1990 to compete in Formula Lotus, a championship he also won. He did the same a year later in British Formula Three.

In 1993, after a short stint in Formula 3000, Barrichello joined the Jordan Formula One team and a series of impressive drives in an uncompetitive car only enhanced his reputation.

A crash during practice at the 1994 San Marino Grand Prix almost killed him when his car left the track and flew into a retaining fence. It was a tragic weekend for the sport as Roland Ratzenberger and Ayrton Senna were both killed. Barrichello recovered and eventually finished sixth in the championship.

He spent three barren years with Stewart Grand Prix from 1997 to 1999, although he did finish seventh in the championship in his last year. He then signed for Ferrari for the next six years, although he was hired primarily in a supporting role to the all-conquering Michael Schumacher. Team orders saw him relinquish a number of certain victories and he'd had enough by the end of the 2005 season.

Barrichello moved to Honda alongside Jenson Button for 2006 but he had a poor season. The following year was equally unproductive and he failed to score any points. 2008 was another difficult season, although he did break Riccardo Patrese's record for the number of GP starts (256), and he scored one podium finish at Silverstone. The Honda team collapsed at the end of the year but the remnants morphed into Brawn GP.

With a competitive car underneath him, Barrichello drove like a man possessed and scored two wins and a further four podiums, leaving him third in the championship behind Button and Sebastian Vettel. He then moved to Williams but the following two seasons were not as successful and he retired from F1 before the 2012 campaign.

Name: Rubens Gonçalves BARRICHELLO
Nationality: Brazilian
Born: 23rd May 1972
Seasons: 1993-2011
Team/manufacturer(s): Jordan, Stewart, Ferrari, Honda, Brawn, Williams
Grand Prix: 326
Race wins: 11
Championship wins: 0

Berger

Gerhard Berger began racing Alfa Suds but soon graduated to Formula Three, where he proved himself a driver of considerable talent. By 1984, he'd caught the attention of the Formula One teams and he was offered a drive with ATS at his home grand prix.

The following season he signed for Arrows but they were an under-funded team and he made little impact. His career took off in 1986 with Benetton and he won his first grand prix in Mexico. This brought him to the attention of Ferrari, a top-tier team that allowed him to win the Italian Grand Prix only weeks after the death of Enzo Ferrari.

Berger signed up as Ayrton Senna's team-mate at McLaren from 1990 to 1992, and he ably supported the Brazilian in his title-winning seasons. Ferrari were still struggling, however, so Berger was re-hired to help change their fortune. The Austrian delivered, winning at Hockenheim, the team's first victory for

Above: *Gerhard Berger of Austria drives the Ferrari in the rain*

three years. When Michael Schumacher joined the team, Berger felt he would be overlooked so he went back to Benetton and helped himself to another win at Hockenheim in 1997.

Berger retired at the end of the season to become competitions' director for BMW. He also invested in the fledgling Scuderia Toro Rosso team.

Name: Gerhard BERGER
Nationality: Austrian
Born: 27th August 1959
Seasons: 1984-1997
Team/manufacturer(s): ATS, Arrows, Benetton, Ferrari, McLaren
Grand Prix: 210
Race wins: 10
Championship wins: 0

Bordino

BORDINO

Right: *Bordino's wrecked Bugatti at the 1928 Alessandria GP*

Below: *Bordino with his Fiat at the 1922 French GP*

Pietro Bordino was reckoned by Henry Seagrave, amongst others, to be the fastest driver in the 1920s. He began racing a Fiat at hill-climbs in 1908 but didn't make an impact on the sport until after the war when he set the fastest laps at the Italian and French GPs.

In 1922 he won the di Vetturette and Italian GPs, the latter at the new Monza circuit, but he then endured a few quiet years before bouncing back to win the Milan GP. While practising for the 1928 Alessandria GP, his car struck a dog at full speed and he drowned after crashing into the River Tarano.

Name: Pietro BORDINO
Nationality: Italian
Born: 22nd November 1887
Died: 22nd April 1928
Seasons: 1908-1928
Team/manufacturer(s): Fiat, Bugatti
Race wins: 3
Championship wins: 0

Boutsen

Thierry Boutsen made a name for himself in 1978 when he won 15 of 18 races in the Formula Ford 1600 championship. A move to Formula Three soon followed and he came second in the 1980 championship, a position he equalled in Formula Two in 1981.

Despite these early successes, he wasn't hired on talent alone and could only make it onto the grid for the 1983 Formula One season by paying $500,000 for a drive with Arrows. After impressing with his outright speed and reliability, he was signed by Benetton in 1987 and Williams in 1989. In his first year driving for Sir Frank Williams, he won both the Canadian and the Australian Grands Prix. The following year he won the Hungarian Grand Prix.

Boutsen finished his career with Ligier then Jordan before retiring at the end of the 1993 season. He raced sportscars until a bad crash at Le Mans in 1999 saw him step down from top-flight motorsport.

Above: *Thierry Boutsen of Belgium.*

Name: Thierry BOUTSEN
Nationality: Belgian
Born: 13th July 1957
Seasons: 1983–1993
Team/manufacturer(s): Arrows, Benetton, Williams, Ligier and Jordan
Grand Prix: 164
Race wins: 3
Championship wins: 0

Brabham

Jack Brabham's father was a keen motorist and taught Jack to drive when he was only 12. He left school at 15 and worked in a garage repairing cars. Keen to get ahead in this profession, he spent his evenings studying engineering at college.

He served in the air force during the war but then returned home to start his own car repair business. One of his customers was an American, Johnny Schonberg, who raced midgets. Brabham helped prepare his car but Schonberg's wife persuaded her husband to give up racing. Somewhat by default, Brabham inherited the car so he decided to race it himself.

Despite his inexperience, Brabham won the New South Wales Championship in his first season, during which he teamed up with long-term engineer Ron Tauranac. The pair moved to England in 1955 and Brabham made his debut at the Aintree Grand Prix driving his own Maserati 250F. He then joined the Cooper team, where he proved himself a driver of immense talent and courage, and he duly won the Formula One title in 1959 and 1960.

As good as the Coopers were, Brabham decided to build his own car with Tauranac. A limit on engine size (1500cc) did not suit Brabham's aggressive style and he failed to win any races in the 1961 season. However, team-mate Dan Gurney gave the Brabham team its first victory at Rouen in 1964.

Brabham's luck changed in 1966 when the rules were changed to allow engines

Above: Brabham in a Brabham Repco at Silverstone

up to 3000cc. He sourced an engine from Repco and, in its first year, the new car took Brabham to victory at the French, British, Dutch and German Grands Prix. He therefore became the first – and so far only – driver to win the Formula One World Championship in a car bearing his own name.

Brabham wanted to retire in 1970 but he couldn't sign a driver good enough to take his place. He began the season with a win at the South African Grand Prix but announced his retirement aged 44 after the final round in Mexico.

He returned to his garage business in Australia and made several appearances at historic car events. He was knighted in 1978 for services to motorsport, a sport in which all three of his sons have been also involved.

Name: Sir John Arthur (Jack) BRABHAM OBE
Nationality: Australian
Born: 2nd April 1926
Seasons: 1955-1970
Team/manufacturer(s): Cooper, Rob Walker, Brabham
Grand Prix: 128
Race wins: 14
Championship wins: 3

Brooks

Tony Brooks was the son of a dentist. While studying to follow in his father's footsteps, he started racing a Healey in club events in 1952. Three years later, he drove a Formula Two car at Crystal Palace and, although he only finished fourth, he managed to beat three Formula One cars. He then travelled to Sicily to race in a non-championship grand prix for Connaught. He won the event and became the first British driver since 1924 to win a continental race in a British car.

Brooks signed for BRM in 1956 but crashed on debut at Silverstone when his car's throttle jammed open. Having then joined Vanwall, he scored notable wins in Belgium, Germany and Italy, which gave him third place in the 1958 championship behind Mike Hawthorn and Stirling Moss. It was a tragic year for the sport, however, with four drivers killed at events and Hawthorn dying after a crash in his Jaguar on the Guildford bypass.

A move to Ferrari in 1959 brought

Brooks wins in France and Germany and he finished second in that year's championship to great rival Jack Brabham. He continued racing in Formula One until 1961, by which time he was concentrating more on his garage business in Weybridge.

Name: Charles Anthony Stanford (Tony) BROOKS
Nationality: British
Born: 25th February 1932
Seasons: 1956-1961
Team/manufacturer(s): BRM, Vanwall, Ferrari, Cooper
Grand Prix: 39
Race wins: 5
Championship wins: 0

Brundle

artin Brundle was born in Norfolk, where he started racing on grass tracks before graduating to hot rods. He came to attention of the motorsport press and public, however, when he tussled with Ayrton Senna for the British Formula Two Championship in 1983.

This epic duel (which Senna won at the last race of the season) saw both drivers promoted to Formula One the following year, with Brundle joining Tyrrell. In his first race, in Brazil, he finished in fifth place, while at Detroit he came second behind Nelson Piquet.

Brundle never managed to get the car his talent deserved and he regularly moved between teams. Despite strong performances, including five podium finishes in 1992 with Benetton, he never reached the top step and retired at the end of 1996.

Brundle was a top-class sportscars driver and he became world champion in 1988. Two years later he won at Le Mans in a Jaguar.

He retired from the track in 2001 but then forged a career as a commentator for ITV, while he also acted as David Coulthard's manager.

Name: Martin BRUNDLE
Nationality: British
Born: 1st June 1959
Seasons: 1984–1989, 1991–1996
Team/manufacturer(s): Tyrrell, Zakspeed, Williams, Brabham, Benetton, Ligier, McLaren, Jordan
Grand Prix: 161
Race wins: 0
Championship wins: 0

Button

Below: *Jenson Button celebrates his first ever Formula One victory*

Jenson Button began karting at the age of eight. With the support of his father, John (a rally-cross driver), the youngster annihilated the opposition in the 1991 British Cadet Kart Championship when he won all 34 races.

He then took the British Open Kart Championship three times and, in 1995, he won the Italian ICA Senior title. Two years later, he became the youngest winner of the European Supercup, and he also won the Ayrton Senna Memorial Cup in Japan.

In 1998, Button moved to Formula Ford. He took the British Championship with nine wins, was runner-up in the European Championship and won the Formula Ford Festival. The following year he graduated to Formula Three and made an instant impact, taking pole position for the first race of the season. He promptly finished third in the championship and earned the Rookie of the Year award.

He also tested for the Prost GP team and outpaced the more experienced Jean Alesi. Williams heard about his precocious talent and signed him for the following season alongside Ralf Schumacher.

Button's first year in Formula One was moderately successful: he won a point at his second race in Brazil, thus becoming the youngest British driver to score a championship point. He finished the season in eighth overall.

In 2001, Button moved to Benetton but he struggled with a new car. The team was re-branded Renault for the 2002 championship and he returned a number of solid performances to finish the year in seventh place.

Button then signed for BAR Honda alongside Jacques Villeneuve but the two didn't get on and he had to play second-fiddle to his more experienced team-mate. His second year with BAR was more productive even though he didn't win a race. He scored consistently and was on the podium ten times. He eventually finished third in the championship behind the all-conquering Ferraris of Michael Schumacher and Rubens Barrichello.

If 2004 had been a career highlight, 2005 was the opposite. He ended the season ninth after being disqualified in San Marino for having a reserve fuel tank concealed within the main tank. The team was penalised with a two-race ban, ending any hope of him challenging for the title, although he did score points in each of the last ten races.

In 2006, Button signed for Williams but he backed out of the deal when he learned that BMW would not be supplying the engines. The season saw him notch two podiums and several fourth-placed finishes but a number of retirements meant he could only finish mid-table.

Button struggled in an uncompetitive Honda throughout 2007 and 2008 and, when the team folded at the end of his second season, he thought he would be left without a seat. Thankfully, Ross Brawn revitalised the team and provided Button and Rubens Barrichello with competitive cars for 2009.

Button duly delivered, winning six of the first seven races, but poor performances mid-season saw the title slipping from his grasp. A Red Bull resurgence meant Vettel was also pressing for the driver honours but Button drove

Above: *Jenson Button in action during F1 pre-season testing at the Circuit de Catalunya in 2006*

an inspired race in Brazil and took the championship with a round to spare. He then joined McLaren alongside Lewis Hamilton but he didn't make much of an impact until 2011 when he scored two wins and a further eight podiums, eventually finishing runner-up to Vettel. The following season he was inconsistent, scoring three wins and the same number of podiums, but several poor results saw him finish fifth in the championship.

Name: Jenson Alexander Lyons BUTTON
Nationality: British
Born: 19th January 1980
Seasons: 2000-
Team/manufacturer(s): Williams, Benetton/Renault, BAR, Honda, Brawn GP, McLaren
Grand Prix: 230
Race wins: 15
Championship wins: 1

Caracciola

Rudi Caracciola was born in Remagen and developed a taste for driving fast cars while working as an apprentice at the Fafnir car factory. He joined Mercedes and won two hill-climbing championships with the silver arrows before moving to Alfa Romeo in 1932. He crashed while practising for the Monaco GP and broke his thigh so badly, however, that he was sidelined for more than a year.

He returned with Mercedes-Benz and won three European titles (the equivalent of the F1 world championship) in 1935, 1937 and 1938. He crashed heavily during qualifying for the 1946 Indy 500 when a bird struck him in the head and partially paralysed him. A second comeback was ruled out when he crashed again in a sportscar race in Berne.

With at least one win at every continental GP, including six wins at his home race (which remains a record), Caracciola, the rain master, also broke a class land speed record by hitting nearly 270mph on public roads (also still a record), and he ranks among the greatest of all drivers. He died of liver failure in 1959 and was buried in Switzerland.

Name: Rudolf 'Rudi' CARACCIOLA
Nationality: German
Born: 30th January 1901
Died: 28th September 1959
European championship seasons: 1931-1932, 1935-1939, 1946-1952
Team/manufacturer(s): Mercedes, Alfa Romeo
Grand Prix: 24
Race wins: 10
European championship wins: 3

Cheever

Eddie Cheever was born in Arizona but grew up in Rome, where he began racing karts at an early age. By 15, he'd won the Italian and the European championships. Two years later, he was making a name for himself in Formula Three and the following season he graduated to Formula Two. He was tipped for F1 superstardom but a seat at Ferrari was taken by Gilles Villeneuve. Cheever had to make do with the less promising Theodore team instead.

In 1978, Cheever failed to qualify for his first race in Argentina and the early promise seemed to be an illusion. For the next few years he switched from one team to the next but never had any real success until he scored three podium finishes with Ligier. In 1983 he joined Renault alongside Alain Prost and achieved four more podiums and 22 points overall but he couldn't improve further and retired in 1989.

Cheever also raced in the American

CART series and won the Indy 500 in 1998 in his own car. He joined the GP Masters series in 2006 and won at Silverstone.

Above: *Eddie Cheever before the Brazilian Grand Prix*

Name: Edward McKay (Eddie) CHEEVER
Nationality: American
Born: 10th January 1958
Seasons: 1978, 1980-1089
Team/manufacturer(s): Theodore, Hesketh, Osella, Tyrrell, Ligier, Renault, Alfa Romeo, Haas Lola, Arrows
Grand Prix: 143
Race wins: 0
Championship wins: 0

Chiron

Louis Chiron learned to drive as a youngster but didn't join the grand prix circus until after the war (he was a chauffeur to Marshals Pétain and Foch). He won his first race near Toulouse in 1926 and won a further three GPs in a Bugatti before switching to Alfa Romeo. He won his home GP five times, the Czechoslovakian GP three times and the Spanish, Marne, German, Italian, Belgian and Monaco races at least once each.

He also won the prestigious Monte Carlo Rally in 1954 and, after a career spanning 35 years in which he chalked up the record as the oldest F1 driver (58), he remains one of the greatest French drivers of all time.

Name: Louis CHIRON
Nationality: French
Born: 3rd August 1899
Died: 22nd June 1979
Seasons: 1950-1951, 1953, 1955-1956, 1958
Team/manufacturer(s): Maserati, Alfa Romeo, Ecurie Rosier, Lancia, Scuderia Centro Sud
Race wins: 16
Championship wins: 0

Clark

Jim Clark grew up on a farm in Scotland and enjoyed racing bicycles and cars from an early age. He first sampled competition when rallying in local events and initially entered his own Sunbeam Talbot. His first big win came in 1957 in a Porsche 356 1600 Super, when he took the Border Motor Racing Club Trophy. Before long, he was driving a Jaguar D-Type for the Borders Reivers Team.

In 1959, Clark tested a Lotus Formula Two car and returned times comparable with Graham Hill despite not having any experience in single-seat cars. Lotus signed Clark immediately but steered him into Formula Two. His talent couldn't be ignored, however, and he made the switch to Formula One when Hill moved to BRM.

Clark soon made a name for himself, scoring points at his second grand prix (Spa) by finishing fifth. Sadly, several crashes that weekend resulted in the deaths of Alan Stacey and Chris Bristow, and severe injuries to Stirling Moss.

The following season was also marred by tragedy. A collision between Clark and the Ferrari of Wolfgang von Trips at Monza led to the latter's car careering into the crowd. Von Trips and 15 spectators were killed. Although Clark knew the accident wasn't his fault, he was still drawn into a lengthy enquiry.

The following year Clark finished second in the championship (three wins) and in 1963 he finally took the drivers' title with seven wins and 54 points. In 1964 and 1965, Clark won another nine races, with the latter year seeing him crowned champion for the second time despite him missing the Monaco Grand

Above: *Jim Clark wins the British Grand Prix at Silverstone*

Prix in favour of the Indy 500. He was the first driver to win the blue riband event in a mid-engined car, and the only driver to win both the Indy 500 and the F1 world championship in the same year.

With Lotus struggling under new regulations, he wasn't as competitive the following year and he finished the season in sixth place. In 1967, however, the new Lotus 49 with its three-litre Cosworth V8 gave him another four wins and third place in the championship.

The 1968 season began with Clark taking his 25th Formula One victory. He then travelled to Hockenheim in Germany to compete in a Formula Two race on 7th April but his car left the track during testing and hit a tree at high speed. Clark was killed instantly, a tragic end to a career that saw him lauded as one of the great geniuses of motorsport alongside Fangio, Moss and Senna. The accident was probably caused by a deflating rear tyre and not by driver error.

Name: James (Jim) CLARK
Nationality: British
Born: 4th March 1936
Died: 7th April 1968
Seasons: 1960-1968
Team/manufacturer(s): Lotus
Grand Prix: 73
Race wins: 25
Championship wins: 2

Collins

Peter Collins's father worked in the motor trade and his son served an apprenticeship at Ford's Dagenham plant. He enjoyed a successful stint in 500cc Formula Three before switching to Formula Two in 1952 where he ended up sharing a drive with Stirling Moss at HWM. The pair raced successfully across Europe, and Collins competed in five Formula One races. The following season he only drove at three events but he had little success and left the team for Vanwall, then Maserati and, finally, Ferrari.

He immediately saw results, finishing second at Monaco and winning in Belgium and France. There was a good chance he could have challenged for the championship that year but he donated his car to team leader Fangio in Italy to give the maestro a shot at the title.

Collins's last Formula One win came at the 1958 British Grand Prix. He crashed at the German Grand Prix while battling for the lead and died from his injuries later the same day.

Above: *Peter Collins in the Ferrari in which he won the British Grand Prix at Silverstone*

Name: Peter John COLLINS
Nationality: British
Born: 6th November 1931
Died: 3rd August 1958
Seasons: 1952-1958
Team/manufacturer(s): HWM, Vanwall, Maserati, Ferrari
Grand Prix: 35
Race wins: 3
Championship wins: 0

Coulthard

David Coulthard was brought up in the southwest of Scotland where his father ran a haulage company. A keen karter, David progressed rapidly and, by the time he was 12, he was the Scottish Junior Kart Champion, a title he won five years running. In 1986 and 1987, he also took the British Super Kart One Championship.

He was soon racing in Formula Ford, and he won both the Dunlop/Autosport and P&O Ferries Junior Championships in his first year. This brought him to the attention of the wider motosports community and he received the McLaren/Autosport Young Driver of the Year award.

The following season, Coulthard competed in Formula Vauxhall Lotus and the GM Lotus Euroseries. He came fourth and fifth respectively and then graduated to British Formula Three. His star was on the rise and he moved up to Formula 3000 for two moderately successful seasons before winning the GT class at Le Mans in 1992.

Coulthard was invited to test for Benetton and Williams, and he signed for the latter as their official test driver for the 1994 season. He would have continued in Formula 3000 but fate intervened when Ayrton Senna was killed at San Marino. Coulthard was drafted in as the Brazilian's replacement (alongside Damon Hill) and his Formula One career was up and running.

He played second fiddle to Hill in his first season and also had to let ex-champion Nigel Mansell drive at four events, but he still managed to impress and took second place at Estoril as well as finishing eighth in the championship.

He was given the race seat for 1995 but, despite winning in Portugal, he ended up supporting Hill's title charge. He still took third place in the championship and would have done better were it not for a few uncharacteristic mistakes.

Coulthard moved to McLaren in 1996 and took seventh place in the championship. This ushered in a six-year period where Coulthard won several races and was often in contention for the championship. He won two grands prix in 1997 and finished the season in third place.

In 1998, Coulthard and team-mate Mika Häkkinen had the best machinery, although the latter went on to win the championship while Coulthard had to settle for third place, a position he matched in 2000. He came closest to the title the following season, although this time Michael Schumacher stood in his way. His performances then tailed off and he left McLaren at the end of 2004.

He joined Red Bull in 2005 to give the team some experience but he struggled for pace and, despite a number of low-scoring finishes, he only managed a podium in Monaco and another in Canada over the next four years. He retired at the end of the 2008 season and took a role as a television commentator and analyst.

Name: David Marshall COULTHARD
Nationality: British
Born: 27th March 1971
Seasons: 1994-2008
Team/manufacturer(s): Williams, McLaren, Red Bull
Grand Prix: 247
Race wins: 13
Championship wins: 0

De Angelis

Right: *Elio de Angelis before the 1982 Dutch GP at Zandvoort*

Elio de Angelis came from a wealthy Italian family with the resources to help him from an early career in karting to Formula Three by the time he was 19. He won his third race and went on to take the Italian Championship in 1977 so he clearly had talent too.

After a brief spell in Formula Two, De Angelis signed for the under-funded Shadow team in 1979 and surprised everyone by claiming fourth place at the US Grand Prix. He was then signed by Lotus, where he remained until 1985, regularly scoring points as well as winning in Austria in 1982 and San Marino in 1985.

After a move to Brabham in 1986, De Angelis was testing at Paul Ricard in France when the car's rear wing came off, the loss of downforce causing it to crash. Although not seriously injured, De Angelis couldn't get out of the car and died in hospital from smoke inhalation.

Name: Elio DE ANGELIS
Nationality: Italian
Born: 26th March 1958
Died: 15th May 1986
Seasons: 1979-1986
Team/manufacturer(s): Shadow, Lotus, Brabham
Grand Prix: 109
Race wins: 2
Championship wins: 0

De Cesaris

Andrea de Cesaris was born in Rome. An early move into go-kart racing saw him crowned world champion and he joined British Formula Three aged 18 in 1977.

De Cesaris drove for Alfa Romeo in two GPs at the end of the 1980 season, but he failed to finish in either the Canadian or American events and gained a reputation for being reckless (he crashed in the latter). In 1984, now driving for McLaren, he crashed or span out in six of 14 races and earned the nickname 'De Crasheris'.

He slowly matured into a quiet and competent driver, however, although he still managed to destroy his Ligier at the 1985 Austrian Grand Prix, an incident for which he was then fired. De Cesaris moved first to Minardi and then Brabham before signing for Rial in 1988. He enjoyed a good season and finished fourth at the US East Grand Prix. He wasn't retained, however, and flirted with several teams before retiring at the end of the 1994 season. He finished on a low note by spinning off in his last race.

De Cesaris retired to Monte Carlo to work as a currency broker but he briefly returned to racing in the 2006 GP Masters alongside Nigel Mansell and Derek Warwick, amongst others.

Name: Andrea DE CESARIS
Nationality: Italian
Born: 31st May 1959
Seasons: 1980-1994
Team/manufacturer(s): Porsche, Maserati, Cooper
Grand Prix: 214
Race wins: 0
Championship wins: 0

Above: Andrea de Cesaris

De La Rosa

Right: *De la Rosa tests for McLaren in Spain in 2008*

Born in Barcelona in 1971, Pedro de la Rosa began his career with model cars, and he was twice European Radio-controlled Car Off-road Champion in the 1980s. He then moved to racing karts before becoming Spanish Formula Fiat Uno Champion in 1989.

A year later, he was Spanish Formula Ford Champion, and in 1992 he won both the European and the British Formula Renault Championships. In 1995, he was Japanese Formula Three Champion and in 1997 he won the Formula Nippon F3000 Championship and Japan All GT Championship.

This brought him to the attention of Jordan and he signed to test for the team in 1998. Arrows gave him a race seat but he had limited success and left for Jaguar the following year. It was another tough season so he spent the next two years testing for McLaren. In 2005, he was given the chance to drive for the team at the Bahrain Grand Prix and he finished an impressive fifth. The following season he only raced in five grands prix but he finished three, including a fantastic second to Jenson Button in Hungary.

De la Rosa continued testing for McLaren until late 2009 when he signed to drive for Sauber in the following year's championship. He finished seven of 13 races and scored points in Hungary. He only drove once in 2011 before moving to HRT for the next campaign. It was a disappointing series though as he couldn't finish better than 17th.

Name: Pedro DE LA ROSA
Nationality: Spanish
Born: 24th February 1971
Seasons: 1999-2002, 2005-2006, 2010-
Team/manufacturer(s): Arrows, Jaguar, McLaren, BMW Sauber, HRT
Grand Prix: 107
Race wins: 0
Championship wins: 0

Depailler

Patrick Depailler wanted to be a dental technician but he was distracted by motorbike and car racing, for which he had an inexhaustible talent. He began racing in Lotus Sevens before winning the French Formula Three title in 1971.

He moved to Formula Two for the 1972 season, a year in which he also made his F1 debut at the French GP in a Tyrrell. He also finished seventh in the USA. After a brief return to Formula Two, Depailler became a consistent scorer for Tyrrell, his first victory coming at Monaco in 1978.

Depailler then moved to Ligier and enjoyed a good start to the season. He won in Spain but a hang-gliding accident prevented him from finishing the season. A move to Alfa Romeo saw him struggling with less competitive cars and he crashed heavily when his suspension failed during a test at Hockenheim. He died of head injuries when the car struck the Armco and flipped upside down.

Name: Patrick André Eugène Joseph DEPAILLER
Nationality: French
Born: 9th August 1944
Died: 1st August 1980
Seasons: 1972, 1974-1980
Team/manufacturer(s): Tyrrell, Ligier, Alfa Romeo
Grand Prix: 95
Race wins: 2
Championship wins: 0

Above: *Patrick Depailler of France on his way to finishing third in the Monaco Formula One Grand Prix*

Fangio

Right: *Juan Fangio with his cup after winning the British Grand Prix at Silverstone*

The son of an Italian immigrant, Juan Manuel Fangio cut his teeth on gruelling long-distance road races in South America. After the war, the Argentinean government sponsored him so he travelled to Europe and won six races against the continent's best in a Maserati.

Alfa Romeo recruited him for the 1950 season and he repaid the faith by finishing second in the inaugural championship. The following year he won three races and came second twice, securing the first of his five championship titles.

Fangio moved back to Maserati for 1952 and started the season well but, having driven overnight from England to make the grid for the Italian Grand Prix, his reactions weren't sharp enough to control the Maserati when it went into a slide. The car hit a bank and somersaulted, throwing Fangio out and breaking his neck. He spent so long recuperating that he didn't race again that year.

By his extremely high standards, 1953

was a poor season and he only managed a single win for Maserati. Despite this, several good placings saw him finish the championship in second place. He signed for Mercedes in 1954 and won six out of eight grands prix, and with it the championship. He repeated his success in 1955 alongside team-mate Stirling Moss.

Fangio then moved to Ferrari and took the championship once more with three wins and two second places. He returned to Maserati in 1957 and enjoyed his finest moment at the Nüburbring when a

bungled pit-stop left him nearly a minute behind the Ferraris of Mike Hawthorn and Peter Collins. Instead of settling for third place, Fangio, in an underpowered car, obliterated the lap record time and again. On the penultimate lap he passed the Ferraris and won by three seconds. With his closest title challenger finishing in fourth place, Fangio claimed his fifth drivers' title. It was the drive of a genius and is consistently ranked as the greatest moment in motorsport history.

He retired in 1958 after the French Grand Prix, where Mike Hawthorn slowed to let Fangio's about-to-be-lapped Maserati finish before him as a mark of respect. Fangio got out of his car and simply said: "It's finished." He then returned to Argentina to run a Mercedes dealership.

Fangio died in Buenos Aires in 1995 at the age of 84. He will always be remembered as one of the finest drivers along with Senna, Clark, Nuvolari, Schumacher and Moss. Unlike these other great names, however, one statistic from his career is unlikely to be bettered: he won 24 of the 51 F1 races he entered.

Name: Juan Manuel FANGIO
Nationality: Argentinean
Born: 24th June 1911
Died: 17th July 1995
Seasons: 1950-1951, 1953-1958
Team/manufacturer(s): Alfa Romeo, Maserati, Mercedes, Ferrari
Grand Prix: 52
Race wins: 24
Championship wins: 5

Farina

Nino Farina worked as an engineer before he started competing in hill-climbs in the 1920s. He progressed to circuit racing with Maserati, before joining Alfa Romeo as second driver to the incomparable Tazio Nuvolari. Racing in the Voiturette class, he was Italian champion three times from 1937 to 1939. Then, in 1940, he won the Tripoli Grand Prix.

After the Second World War, he won the 1948 Monaco Grand Prix in a private Maserati, and he continued this success in his first Formula One season. He won three of the six races and became the first F1 world champion.

In his second year he finished well behind Fangio, Ascari and Gonzalez, although he did win at Belgium and finished on the podium in Switzerland, Italy and Spain. In 1952 he moved to Ferrari but had to wait until the Nürburgring the following season to card his first win for the team.

After two unsuccessful years, Farina retired from Formula One, although he did drive in the Indy 500 in 1956. He crashed out of the race and retired from all motorsport soon after. Somewhat ironically, Farina was killed in a car crash on his way to watch the 1966 French Grand Prix.

Name: Emilio Giuseppe (Nino) FARINA
Nationality: Italian
Born: 30th October 1906
Died: 30th June 1966
Seasons: 1950-1955
Team/manufacturer(s): Alfa Romeo, Ferrari
Grand Prix: 34
Race wins: 5
Championship wins: 1

Fisichella

Giancarlo Fisichella was born in Rome and took up karting at an early age. He graduated to Formula Three in his late teens and won the Italian Championship in 1994. After a brief foray into touring cars, he joined the Minardi Formula One team but soon moved to Jordan and then to Benetton (which eventually became Renault). He struggled in uncompetitive cars and could only finish mid-table so he rejoined Jordan for 2002 and 2003.

Fisichella won his first grand prix, albeit in controversial circumstances, at a very wet Interlagos in Brazil. The weather and several accidents forced stewards to end the race at the end of lap 55, but as Fisichella had just overtaken Räikkönen there was some confusion as to who had won and the result wasn't decided in the Italian's favour until several days later. But Fisichella won again in Australia in 2005 and eventually finished a creditable fifth in the championship. His third and final win came for Renault in Malaysia in 2006. In his best season to date, he finished fourth in the drivers' standings but the departure of team-mate Fernando Alonso saw the team's fortunes slide and 2007 was a poor season.

When Alonso returned in 2008, Fisichella moved to Force India but the car's handling let it down and he failed to score a point. Despite a superb second place at Belgium the following year, and a brief stint with Ferrari, Fisichella was not retained and he retired from F1 at the end of the 2009 season.

Above: Giancarlo Fisichella in action during practice for the Formula One Brazilian Grand Prix

Name: Giancarlo FISICHELLA
Nationality: Italian
Born: 14th January 1973
Seasons: 1996-2009
Team/manufacturer(s): Minardi, Jordan, Benetton, Sauber, Renault, Force India, Ferrari
Grand Prix: 231
Race wins: 3
Championship wins: 0

Fittipaldi

Emerson Fittipaldi came from racing stock: his parents both raced and his father was also a well-known journalist and motorsport commentator. Along with his brother, Wilson, he founded a car spares business to raise money to further their karting careers, and Emerson was Brazilian Kart Champion by the age of 18.

He then moved to Formula Vee, a championship he won in 1967. This persuaded him to abandon a mechanical engineering course and move to England to buy a Formula Ford car. He enjoyed immediate success and graduated to Formula Three. His skill and courage soon caught the eye of Lotus supremo Colin Chapman who was looking for a new driver.

Fittipaldi made his Formula One debut at the 1970 British Grand Prix. He performed well and backed it up with solid drives in Germany and Austria. Fittipaldi was shaken but unhurt after a high-speed crash at Monza but the weekend got much worse when team-mate Jochen Rindt was killed in a practice accident. The team's third driver, John Miles, was badly shaken by the news and retired immediately. This left a relative novice as team leader but Fittipaldi got on with the business of racing and won his next race in the USA.

The 1971 season was a washout because Fittipaldi had been injured in a road accident, although he did manage three podium finishes. However, by 1972 he was ready to challenge for the title and he duly won five of the 12 races. Aged just 25, he became the youngest champion in history, and the team also secured the constructors' championship. Lotus collected the constructors'

Left: *Lotus team leader Emerson Fittipaldi rounds a bend at Brands Hatch*

championship again the following year, and although Fittipaldi put up a spirited defence of his individual title, his season tapered off after a strong start and he was beaten by Jackie Stewart.

Fittipaldi left Lotus for McLaren in 1974. He won three more races and clinched the championship for a second time. Two wins and four second places almost gave him a third drivers' title but he eventually finished the 1975 season behind Ferrari's Niki Lauda.

He then moved to the team run by his brother but Fittipaldi couldn't compete with the likes of Ferrari, Lotus and Williams. Despite this, he stayed with the team for five years and only retired in 1980, although he continued to manage the outfit until it folded in

1982. He then returned to Brazil to run the family business.

Fittipaldi was back behind the wheel during the American CART series in 1994. He continued to compete until 1996 but a bad accident forced him to retire again. He briefly came out of retirement to race in the 2005 GP Masters.

Name: Emerson FITTIPALDI
Nationality: Brazilian
Born: 12th December 1946
Seasons: 1970–1980
Team/manufacturer(s): Lotus, McLaren, Fittipaldi
Grand Prix: 149
Race wins: 14
Championship wins: 2

Frentzen

Right: *Frentzen steers his car as rain falls on the Silverstone racetrack, 14 July 2001*

The son of a funeral director, Heinz-Harald Frentzen began racing karts at the age of 13. By the time he was 18 he had progressed to German Formula Ford 2000 and was runner-up in the 1987 championship. He went on to win the German Formula Opel Lotus Championship in his first season and then joined German Formula Three in 1989. He finished joint second with Michael Schumacher.

Frentzen was immediately signed by Sauber for the 1994 Formula One season. His performances attracted the attention of Frank Williams who was looking to replace Ayrton Senna after the latter's fatal crash early in the season. Frentzen stayed with Sauber through 1996, however, and only moved to Williams in 1997. He won at San Marino and backed it up with two second places and four third-place finishes. In what was a controversial season that saw Michael Schumacher disqualified, Frentzen came second overall behind Jacques Villeneuve.

Frentzen then signed for Jordan and won two races in 1999 (France and Italy). Several podium finishes gave him third place in the championship. Unfortunately, his relationship with Jordan turned sour and he moved to Prost towards the end of the 2001 season. He then joined Arrows in 2002 but the team went bankrupt so he rejoined Sauber until the end of 2003. He couldn't recapture the winning ways so he retired from F1 and joined the German DTM touring car series.

Name: Heinz-Harald FRENTZEN
Nationality: German
Born: 18th May 1967
Seasons: 1994-2003
Team/manufacturer(s): Sauber, Williams, Jordan, Prost, Arrows
Grand Prix: 160
Race wins: 3
Championship wins: 0

Ginther

Born in Hollywood, Richie Ginther didn't start racing MGs until his twenties, but he then drove a Ferrari with Phil Hill to second place in the 1954 Carrera Panamericana. This led to a drive with an American Ferrari importer, and Ginther was soon making an impression in local races.

In the late 1950s, he was offered a works drive by Ferrari so he moved to Italy and discovered a talent for single-seat racing. He stepped up to Formula Two and then to Formula One at the Monaco Grand Prix in 1960. He finished in sixth place and impressed again when he took second at the Italian Grand Prix.

Despite another good season with Ferrari the following year, he was dropped and joined Graham Hill at BRM. In 1963, Ginther finished third in the championship behind his team-mate and Jim Clark. He signed for Honda in 1965 and won his only Formula One race in an underpowered car at the Mexican Grand Prix.

The following season was tough and, after driving just one race for Eagle in 1967, Ginther decided to retire. He managed race teams for a while before returning to travel around North America in a camper van. He died on holiday in France in 1989.

Above: *American driver Richie Ginther (1930 - 1989) racing for Honda at Silverstone*

Name: Richard (Richie) GINTHER
Nationality: American
Born: 5th August 1930
Died: 20th September 1989
Seasons: 1960-1967
Team/manufacturer(s): Ferrari, Scarab, BRM, Honda, Cooper, Eagle
Grand Prix: 54
Race wins: 1
Championship wins: 0

Gonzalez

GONZALEZ

Right: *Jose Froilan Gonzalez with his Grand Prix trophy after a win at Silverstone*

Below: *Gonzalez leading the pack at Silverstone*

Pepe Gonzalez was one of Fangio's great friends and rivals. He hit the headlines in 1951 when he beat team Mercedes at his home GP. The victory earned him a drive with Ferrari and he gave the team its first F1 win over the all-conquering Alfas at the 1951 British Grand Prix, a year in which he delivered consistent points finishes and ended the championship in third place.

He then had two seasons with Maserati but moved back to Ferrari in 1954 to mount another assault on the drivers' title. Four podiums and a win saw him come up just short, but he won numerous non-championship GPs and only retired from F1 after his home event in 1960.

At the time of writing, he is the oldest living winner of a grand prix.

Name: José-Froilan 'Pepe' GONZALEZ
Nationality: Argentinean
Born: 5th October 1922
Seasons: 1950-1957, 1960
Team/manufacturer(s): Maserati, Talbot-Lago, Vanwall, Ferrari
Grand Prix: 26
Race wins: 3
Championship wins: 0

Goux

Jules Goux was a talented Frenchman who made his name driving Peugeots in Sicily, Catalonia and Normandy. He won at Le Mans on the infamous Circuit de la Sarthe in 1912, then travelled to the US and won the 1913 Indy 500 at the Brickyard, the first European to do so. He also finished fourth in 1914 and third in 1919.

At the end of the First World War, Goux joined Ballot and won the Italian GP at Brescia. With Bugatti he cemented his reputation as one of the finest drivers of his generation with victory in the 1926 French and Spanish GPs. He died after an allergic reaction to crab in 1965.

Above: *Goux on his way to winning the 1913 Indy 500, the first European to take the title*

Left: *Jules Goux*

Name: Jules GOUX
Nationality: French
Born: 6th April 1885
Died: 6th March 1965
Seasons: 1906–1926
Team/manufacturer(s): Peugeot, Ballot, Bugatti
Race wins: 3
Championship wins: 0

Gurney

Right: Dan Gurney

Below: *Last-minute adjustments are made to Dan Gurney's 1962 Indy 500 racecar*

Dan Gurney was born in New York but he grew up in California and began racing a Triumph TR2. He soon worked his way up to Formula One and was offered a drive with Ferrari. He impressed from the outset, finishing on the podium twice in his first three races. He left Ferrari at the end of the year and joined BRM but without the financial clout behind him he found little success. He drove for several more teams and won the 1967 Belgian Grand Prix in an Eagle, the last of his four victories.

Gurney started the tradition of spraying champagne from the podium, which he first did at Le Mans in 1967. He is also the inventor of the Gurney flap, a device used on car and aeroplane wings to increase lift or downforce. In addition, he introduced full-face helmets to Formula One and IndyCar.

Name: Daniel Sexton (Dan) GURNEY
Nationality: American
Born: 13th April 1931
Seasons: 1959-1968, 1970
Team/manufacturer(s): Ferrari, BRM, Porsche, Lotus, Brabham, Eagle, McLaren
Grand Prix: 87
Race wins: 4
Championship wins: 0

Häkkinen

Mika Häkkinen started racing karts at the age of five. He won his first race when he was seven and his first championship at 11. He was Finnish karting champion five times.

Häkkinen moved to Formula Ford 1600 and won the Finnish, Swedish and Nordic championships. The following year, he took the Opel Lotus Euroseries Championship and the British GM Euroseries Championship. Graduating to Formula Three, he won the British Championship in 1990.

Häkkinen was snapped up by Lotus F1 in 1991 but the team was on the slide and he could only finish eighth in the championship. He then moved to McLaren as a test driver but was promoted to the race seat over Michael Andretti mid-season. He then out-qualified team-mate Ayrton Senna at the Portuguese Grand Prix.

The Finn was McLaren number one in 1994 and 1995, but he failed to win any

Above: *Mika Häkkinen crosses the finish line at the 2001 British GP at Silverstone*

races and, after a spectacular crash at the Australian Grand Prix in 1995, he needed an emergency tracheotomy to save his life. He stayed with McLaren for the 1996 campaign and finished a creditable fifth in the championship. Despite winning the last race of the 1997 season, he could only manage sixth in the championship.

In 1998, Häkkinen won eight GPs and took the drivers' championship comfortably. His dices with Michael Schumacher were particularly memorable and it seemed a genuine rivalry would develop between the pair. The following season wasn't as straightforward – the McLarens weren't as reliable and Schumacher was on the comeback trail – but Häkkinen still won

three of the first six races and was ahead of Schumacher when the German broke his leg at Silverstone and had to pull out of the championship. Ferrari's Eddie Irvine stepped up to the plate, however, and the championship went to the final race in Japan. Häkkinen duly won to claim back-to-back drivers' titles.

Häkkinen pushed hard for a hat-trick of championships with wins in Spain, Austria, Hungary and at an epic Belgian GP, but, despite also finishing second seven times, he couldn't prevent the German from taking the title.

Häkkinen's last season in Formula One only yielded two wins and he decided that what had initially been a break from the sport was actually retirement. There were rumours of a comeback in 2005 with Williams but he took up German touring car racing instead.

Name: Mika Pauli HÄKKINEN
Nationality: Finnish
Born: 28th September 1968
Seasons: 1991-2001
Team/manufacturer(s): Lotus, McLaren
Grand Prix: 165
Race wins: 20
Championship wins: 2

Hamilton

Lewis Hamilton was making a name for himself in karting from an early age and he earned a place on the McLaren driver development programme after telling Ron Dennis that he would like to drive for him. He was soon signed up and a year later he won the Formula A European Kart Championship.

He then moved to Formula Renault and won the UK championship in 2003. He soon took the 2005 Formula Three Euroseries title after winning 15 of the 20 rounds. Hamilton then stormed to victory in the GP2 series the following year and earned a place in the McLaren team alongside Fernando Alonso in 2007.

Formula One had finally found a new focal point after Michael Schumacher's retirement. Hamilton scored two wins and nine straight podiums to take the championship by the scruff of the neck. No other driver had made such an impact in their first season. Despite two more wins, a mistake by the team in China and a poor drive in Brazil saw him snatch championship defeat from the jaws of victory. F1 provided a steep learning curve and, with the benefit of hindsight, maybe it was a good thing he didn't win at his first attempt.

A well publicised spat with Alonso saw the Spaniard replaced by Heikki Kovalainen and, without the added pressure of racing a former-world-champion team-mate, Hamilton won in Australia, Monaco, Britain, Germany and China, but he still needed a strong finish in Brazil to pip Felipe Massa to the title. With his hopes fading in poor weather, Hamilton passed Glock on the last corner to claim the points he needed and dash Massa's hopes (the Brazilian

Above: *Lewis Hamilton celebrates on the podium*

Above: *Lewis Hamilton drives during the British Formula One Grand Prix at Silverstone*

had already finished and believed he was champion for a few moments).

The next three years were punctuated by blistering highs (a further 12 wins) and devastating lows (disqualification, crashes, mechanical problems and several run-ins with the stewards), and, despite the odd strong start to a season, Hamilton didn't seriously challenge for the title between 2009 and 2012. He left McLaren for a new challenge at

Mercedes in 2013.

Name: Lewis Carl HAMILTON
Nationality: British
Born: 7th January 1985
Seasons: 2007-
Team/manufacturer(s): McLaren, Mercedes
Grand Prix: 110
Race wins: 21
Championship wins: 1

Hawthorn

Mike Hawthorn was brought up surrounded by machinery. His father, Leslie, had raced motorcycles before the Second World War and also ran a garage business in Farnham. By the age of nine, Hawthorn had decided that he was going to be a racing driver, and he spent his spare time at Brooklands imagining what it would be like to drive on the famous banking.

Public school and technical college led to an apprenticeship with a vehicle manufacturer but Hawthorn was restless and took up racing as a hobby. His father indulged him, supplying him with motorcycles and then cars. His racing career blossomed and he became established on the club circuit in a Riley.

In 1952, Hawthorn was offered a seat in a Formula Two race at Goodwood. Up against the likes of Juan Manual Fangio, Hawthorn shocked everyone by winning the race and the subsequent Formula Libre event. He then came second in the

Formula One race despite piloting the underpowered Cooper-Bristol.

Inspired by this success, Hawthorn entered the remaining Formula One races of the season, a championship which was dominated by Ferrari's Alberto Ascari. Wearing his trademark bow tie, Hawthorn finished fourth in Belgium and Holland, and third in the UK, giving him fifth place overall.

Enzo Ferrari promptly hired him for the 1953 season but Hawthorn only managed a last-gasp win over Fangio at the French Grand Prix in Reims and he finished the championship in fourth place. He was badly injured at a race in Sicily the following year, and then his father was killed in a road accident. Disillusioned with the Italian team – the high point was a solitary win at the Spanish Grand Prix – Hawthorn left Ferrari to drive for Vanwall and then BRM.

He made the headlines for the wrong reasons at Le Mans in 1955 when Lance

Macklin swerved to avoid him as he pitted and drove into Pierre Levegh's path. The unlucky Frenchman clipped Macklin's Healey and his Mercedes somersaulted into the crowd, killing more than 80 people. Hawthorn fought an epic duel with Fangio and won the race but he was pilloried for celebrating afterwards and was initially blamed for the incident.

He joined good friend Peter Collins at Ferrari in 1957 but, when Collins was killed at the Nürburgring in 1958, this was the final straw for Hawthorn. He saw out the championship (which Moss all but handed to him out of courtesy) and reluctantly retired.

Hawthorn returned to run the family business in Farnham but he was suffering from severe kidney problems that may have caused him to black out on the Guildford bypass when at the wheel of his Jaguar. The car hit an oncoming truck and left the road before hitting a tree. Hawthorn died from his injuries.

Name: John Michael (Mike) HAWTHORN
Nationality: British
Born: 10th April 1929
Died: 22nd January 1959
Seasons: 1952-1958
Team/manufacturer(s): LD Hawthorn, AHM Bryde, Ferrari, Vanwall, BRM
Grand Prix: 47
Race wins: 3
Championship wins: 1

Heidfeld

Born in Mönchengladbach, Nick Heidfeld started racing karts at the age of 11. Six years later he won eight of nine races and took the German Formula Ford Championship. By 1997, he had won the German Formula Three Championship and, two years later, he took the International Formula 3000 Championship.

Heidfeld joined Prost in 2000 but his first season in Formula One was a disappointment and he scored no points, so he moved to Sauber until the end of 2003. He then spent a largely fruitless year with Jordan before joining Williams in 2005.

The season with Williams was mixed: he enjoyed two early second-place finishes but missed the Italian and Belgian GPs after picking up an injury during testing. His recovery was hampered after he was hit by a motorcycle when he was out cycling. Heidfeld rejoined Sauber for 2006 but only managed one podium finish. He stayed with the team for the following two seasons and enjoyed arguably his best years.

He scored 12 top-four finishes and was fifth overall in 2007. He was sixth the following year having again scored more than 60 points. The 2009 season was less successful and he sat out most of the 2010 campaign. After a promising start to 2011 with new team Lotus, including a podium in Malaysia, he was dropped for the remainder of the season after crashing in Canada and retiring in Hungary when his car caught fire.

Name: Nick HEIDFELD
Nationality: German
Born: 10th May 1977
Seasons: 2000-2011
Team/manufacturer(s): Prost, Sauber, Jordan, Williams, BMW Sauber, Renault
Grand Prix: 185
Race wins: 0
Championship wins: 0

Herbert

Below: *Johnny Herbert*

Johnny Herbert began racing karts at the age of 10. By 1978 he was British Junior Karting Champion and he went on to take the senior championship in 1979 and 1982. The following year he drove in Formula Ford before graduating to Formula Ford 2000. And in 1987 he climbed another rung to Formula Three, where he won the British Championship in his first season.

This led to a test with Benetton but Herbert wasn't signed and he had to spend a year in Formula 3000 instead. During the season he had a bad accident that almost cost him his career, but he finally broke into Formula One with Benetton in 1989. He started strongly and finished fourth in Brazil, but he was dropped midway through the season after failing to qualify for the Canadian GP. He joined Tyrrell at the end of the season but his two races yielded no points.

He was signed by Lotus as a test driver in 1990 but he ended up competing in several races. Sadly, his first three years with the team yielded only two points. He fared slightly better in 1993, but 1994 was another washout and he returned to Benetton in 1995. This time he had a competitive car and Herbert won at Silverstone and Monza while also scoring points at eight other races. He finished the season a creditable fourth with 45 points.

He spent the next two years with Sauber but the car wasn't as good and his results dropped off. A move to Stewart in 1999 saw him claim his last F1 victory at the European Grand Prix. The team was renamed Jaguar for 2000 but he had another disappointing season and promptly retired from Formula One to concentrate on sportscar racing in the American Le Mans Series (where he enjoyed considerable success) as well as commentating for television.

Name: John Paul (Johnny) HERBERT
Nationality: British
Born: 25th June 1964
Seasons: 1989-2000
Team/manufacturer(s): Benetton, Tyrrell, Lotus, Ligier, Sauber, Stewart, Jaguar
Grand Prix: 165
Race wins: 3
Championship wins: 0

Hill, Damon

The son of Formula One legend Graham Hill, Damon was brought up in the motorsport world but he didn't initially take to the sport. Aged 11, however, Hill was in the paddock at Silverstone when he was given a ride on a 50cc Honda and he enjoyed it so much that Graham was persuaded to buy one.

By 1981, Hill was considering a career in motorbike racing but his mother decided it was too dangerous and sent him to the Winfield Racing School at Magny-Cours in France. Hill quickly learnt to drive single-seat racing cars but he was still smitten with the idea of racing bikes until he won a Formula Ford race at Brands Hatch in 1983.

He proved himself an able driver and graduated first to Formula Three and then Formula 3000. He joined Williams as a test driver in 1991 and proved himself equally capable behind the wheel of a Formula One car so he signed for Brabham the following year, although he kept his testing spot with Williams. In 1993 he was offered a race seat alongside Alain Prost. He duly repaid the team's faith by winning three races and finishing on the podium in another seven. He ended up third in the championship behind Prost and archrival Ayrton Senna.

The 1994 season was extremely difficult for the Williams team. Senna's death at San Marino almost forced the team to pull out of the sport and elevated Hill to the number one spot. He bore the responsibility calmly and had a great season, winning six races and coming second in another five. He was just one point behind Michael Schumacher going into the last round of the championship in Australia. If he beat the German in Adelaide, he would claim the title.

Schumacher was leading but Hill was closing the gap and heaping pressure on the German. Schumacher couldn't cope,

Above: Damon Hill of Great Britain

made a mistake, ran wide at the East Terrace Corner and hit a wall. As his car bounced back onto the track, he steered towards Hill to try to keep his position. Hill couldn't avoid the collision and both drivers were forced to retire. Schumacher may have taken the championship but Hill was the moral victor, although he couldn't conceal his disappointment at having the title snatched from his grasp.

Another four wins and five podiums gave him second place behind Schumacher in the 1995 championship, but he finally delivered in 1996 with eight wins and two second places having started every race from the front row of the grid.

Somewhat strangely, Williams dropped Hill for Frentzen the following season so the world champion joined lowly Arrows. The car was uncompetitive, however, and was plagued by mechanical problems for much of the year. He then joined Ralf Schumacher at Jordan and gave the team its first win at Spa. He stayed with the team for 1999 but retirements, crashes and poor performances forced him to retire at the end of the season.

He has since been involved in a number of business ventures, as well as returning to the paddock on commentary duty for television.

Name: Damon Graham Devereux HILL, OBE
Nationality: British
Born: 17th September 1960
Seasons: 1992-1999
Team/manufacturer(s): Brabham, Williams, Arrows, Jordan
Grand Prix: 122
Race wins: 22
Championship wins: 1

Hill, Graham

Graham Hill famously did not pass his driving test until he was 24, yet he went on to become a motorsport legend during the 1960s and 1970s. It all started when he saw an advert for a racing school and paid for four laps of Brands Hatch in a Formula Three Cooper 500. He immediately decided this was the career of choice so he took a job as a mechanic at a similar school. A chance meeting with Colin Chapman saw him hired by Lotus.

He initially maintained the team's Formula Two cars but he was convinced that he should be behind the wheel and persuaded Chapman to give him a seat. He made his Formula One debut in 1958 but moved to BRM when the Lotus proved too unreliable. By 1962 BRM had developed a new V8 and Hill won his first race at Zandvoort. Three more victories and two second places saw him crowned world champion.

Had he not suffered with so many mechanical problems, he might have taken the title more often but he had to make do with second for the next three years, although he did win the Indianapolis 500 in 1966. In 1967 he returned to Lotus alongside Jim Clark. Sadly the Scot lost his life in a Formula Two race mid-season, but this only made Hill more determined to win the championship. Three wins and three runners up spots saw him clinch the drivers' title at the last race.

This marked the beginning of the end of his career. He had limited success in 1969, despite a win at Monaco, but a bad

Above: *Graham Hill in his BRM takes the chequered flag in Monaco*

crash at the US Grand Prix at Watkins Glen saw him thrown from his Lotus 49B. His injuries confined him to a wheelchair but he returned to racing the following season.

After a brief but unremarkable stint at Brabham, Hill founded his own team in 1973. They enjoyed little success, however, and he stood down to give Tony Brise the race seat two years later.

A few months after announcing his retirement, Hill, Brise and four members of the team were killed when Hill's light aircraft crashed in thick fog on its approach to Elstree airfield.

Name: Norman Graham HILL
Nationality: British
Born: 15th February 1929
Died: 29th November 1975
Seasons: 1958-1975
Team/manufacturer(s): Lotus, BRM, Brabham, Hill
Grand Prix: 179
Race wins: 14
Championship wins: 2

Hill, Philip

Born in Florida but brought up in California, the young Phil Hill began racing MGs before moving to England in 1949 to work as a trainee at Jaguar. By 1956, he was driving for Ferrari. Two years later, he made his F1 debut in a Maserati at the French Grand Prix. He finished a creditable seventh before rejoining Ferrari

Hill took his first Formula One win at the Italian Grand Prix in 1960. The following year he won in Italy and Belgium and scored consistently throughout the season. He therefore became world champion, the first American driver to take the title. He continued racing until 1966 but couldn't repeat his success to switched to sportscars.

Name: Philip Toll (Phil) HILL
Nationality: American
Born: 20th April 1927
Died: 28th August 2008
Seasons: 1958-1964, 1966
Team/manufacturer(s): Maserati, Ferrari, Cooper, Porsche, ATS, Lotus, Eagle
Grand Prix: 51
Race wins: 3
Championship wins: 1

Hulme

Denny Hulme grew up on a tobacco farm on New Zealand's South Island. After leaving school, he worked in a garage and raced an MG TF in hill-climbs. He came to England under the 'Driver to Europe' scheme and joined Jack Brabham as a mechanic. He was soon driving for the team in Formula Junior but then graduated to Formula Two with Tyrrell.

He was given a top-flight drive in a Brabham at Monaco in 1965, where he finished eighth. He also scored points by finishing fourth in France and fifth in Holland. The following year he was given a seat for the whole season and he finished with four podiums. Hulme's next season was his best: he won at Monaco and Germany and finished on the podium a further six times, which was enough to clinch the drivers' championship.

He might have taken back-to-back titles had his McLaren's suspension not failed in Mexico at the last race of the 1968 season, but he eventually dropped down to third in the overall standings. He stayed with the team for the remainder of his Formula One career, which lasted until 1974, although with the exception of the odd race win and a strong showing in 1972, he couldn't match his earlier success. He then returned to New Zealand to race touring cars.

It was at the wheel of a touring car at Bathurst in 1992 that Hulme had a heart attack. He managed to bring the car to a stop but was pronounced dead at the scene.

Name: Denis Clive (Denny) HULME
Nationality: New Zealander
Born: 18th June 1936
Died: 4th October 1992
Seasons: 1965-1974
Team/manufacturer(s): Brabham, McLaren
Grand Prix: 112
Race wins: 8
Championship wins: 1

Hunt

James Hunt grew up in Berkshire and had ambitions to become a doctor until a friend took him to a race at Silverstone when he was 18. He decided immediately that this was the career of choice and boasted that he'd be Formula One world champion. He went home and bought a wrecked Mini, which he spent the next two years repairing.

He was a good but accident-prone driver (his nickname was 'Hunt the shunt') but he soon graduated to Formula Ford and Formula Three. He always struggled with pre-race nerves and never looked likely to join a top team until the intervention of his friend, Lord Alexander Hesketh, who decided to start his own team with Hunt as the lead driver.

The pair started off unremarkably in Formula Two and Three but Hesketh soon decided that if they were going to lose money they might as well do it in Formula One. The team was seen as

Above: *Hunt celebrates victory at the 1976 Dutch GP*

a bit of a joke but Hunt put in some spectacular performances and even beat Niki Lauda's Ferrari to win the 1975 Dutch Grand Prix. At the end of the season, however, Hesketh pulled out citing financial trouble.

McLaren had taken note of the young upstart and offered Hunt a drive in 1976. Although Lauda appeared to be running away with the championship, a terrible crash at the Nürburgring saw him sidelined for several races and Hunt made a determined assault on his overall lead. The championship would be decided at the last race in Japan. The weather was appalling and Lauda understandably decided not to risk his life a second time.

Above: *James Hunt of Great Britain in action*

He pulled into the pits and handed Hunt the title, although the Briton initially had no idea he'd become champion.

Hunt couldn't match this achievement and, despite two more years with McLaren and a half-season for Wolf, he retired in 1979. He then worked alongside Murray Walker in the BBC commentary box for fourteen years, with the pair widely praised for their entertaining but well-informed banter.

He proposed to girlfriend Helen Dyson on 15th June 1993 but he died aged 46 after a massive heart attack just hours later.

Name: James Simon Wallis HUNT
Nationality: British
Born: 29th August 1947
Died: 15th June 1993
Seasons: 1973-1979
Team/manufacturer(s): Hesketh, McLaren, Wolf
Grand Prix: 93
Race wins: 10
Championship wins: 1

Ickx

Jacky Ickx was the son of a motorsport journalist so he went to several races with his father. He began his career on a 50cc motorbike and was soon winning championships. He graduated to a Lotus Cortina touring car in 1965 and won the national title. The following year, he made his Formula One debut in Germany but he retired, a result he endured again in 1967. However, in a Cooper-Maserati at Monza, he finished sixth.

Ickx showed enough promise to attract the attention of Enzo Ferrari and he signed for the iconic team in 1968. He won in France and scored well in Belgium, Britain and Italy, and eventually finished the championship in fourth place. A year with Brabham brought two more wins and second place in the drivers' standings, a position he matched having re-signed for Ferrari for the 1970 season. Despite winning a couple more races, he never won the championship and his career wound down over the next decade.

He retired at the end of 1979 to concentrate on sportscar racing. Here he enjoyed more success, taking the Le Mans title six times.

Above: *Jacky Ickx of Belgium*

Name: Jacques Bernard (Jacky) ICKX
Nationality: Belgian
Born: 1st January 1945
Seasons: 1967-1979
Team/manufacturer(s): Cooper, Ferrari, Brabham, McLaren, Williams, Lotus, Wolf, Ensign, Ligier
Grand Prix: 120
Race wins: 8
Championship wins: 0

Ireland

Below: *Ireland driving a Lotus Climax at Zandvoort during the 1960 Dutch GP*

Innes Ireland was born in Yorkshire but raised in Scotland. He trained as an engineer with Rolls Royce and then set up his own engineering business in Surrey.

He began racing in the early 1950s, but only made an impact when he raced sportscars in 1957. Colin Chapman recognised his talent and offered him a drive with the Lotus Formula One team in 1959. He only finished two races in his first season, but both brought him points. His second season was more profitable and he came fourth in the drivers' standings. His only win came at the 1961 US Grand Prix at Watkins Glen, however.

Ireland moved to BRP and then Reg Parnell Racing but his best years were behind him and he retired to become a motoring journalist and part-time trawler skipper. He was also president of the British Racing Drivers Club. He died of cancer in 1993.

Name: Robert McGregor Innes (Innes) IRELAND
Nationality: British
Born: 12th June 1930
Died: 22nd October 1993
Seasons: 1959-1966
Team/manufacturer(s): Lotus, BRP, Reg Parnell Racing
Grand Prix: 53
Race wins: 1
Championship wins: 0

Irvine

Eddie Irvine was born in Newtownards, Northern Ireland. He made a living selling cars and investing the money, which helped his burgeoning racing career.

After a spell in Formula Ford 1600, Irvine moved to Formula Three in 1988 and Formula 3000 a year later. After driving for Jordan in Formula 3000, he was promoted to the Formula One seat at the end of the 1993 season. He gained a reckless 'Irv the Swerve' reputation and failed to impress, but he then became 'Steady Eddie' for his smooth driving when he signed for Ferrari. Only then did he begin to make his mark on the championship.

With team-mate Michael Schumacher injured, Irvine had his best season in 1999 when he won four races and pushed Mika Häkkinen all the way. The Finn took the title in Japan, however, and Irvine's career trailed off after an unsuccessful move to Jaguar.

He built up a vast property portfolio during his racing career to ensure he would be financially secure in retirement.

Above: *Irvine's most successful year with Ferrari, 1999*

Name: Edmund (Eddie) IRVINE
Nationality: British
Born: 10th November 1965
Seasons: 1993-2002
Team/manufacturer(s): Jordan, Ferrari, Jaguar
Grand Prix: 148
Race wins: 4
Championship wins: 0

Jabouille

Right: *Jean-Pierre Jabouille of France stands in the pits before a race*

Jean-Pierre Jabouille worked as an engineer before he began racing and maintaining Formula Three cars in 1967 and 1968. He went on to compete in Formula Two and sportscars, and finished third at Le Mans in both 1973 and 1974.

Williams and Surtees gave him a platform in Formula One but he failed to qualify for any races and seemed to be sliding towards obscurity when Tyrrell gave him a seat for the 1975 French GP. He finished 12th but couldn't break into the big-time and retired in almost every race he started. He moved to Renault for three seasons but was dogged by reliability problems, although he did register wins at the 1979 French GP and 1980 Austrian Grand Prix.

He failed to finish a single race for Ligier in 1981 and retired partway through the season. After spending a few years racing sportscars, Jabouille formed his own team and continued to race in the GT series.

Name: Jean-Pierre JABOUILLE
Nationality: French
Born: 1st October 1942
Seasons: 1974-1975, 1977-1981
Team/manufacturer(s): Williams, Surtees, Tyrrell, Renault, Ligier
Grand Prix: 56
Race wins: 2
Championship wins: 0

Jarier

Born near Paris, Jean-Pierre Jarier was a successful Formula France driver before he graduated to Formula Three in 1970 and Formula Two a year later. He made his F1 debut in 1971 in a borrowed March 701 but he didn't finish the only race he entered.

Two years later, he only finished one race throughout the season so he moved to Shadow for the next three years. Despite a third-place finish at Monaco in 1974, he only recorded two more points' finishes before signing for ATS, Ligier, Lotus and then Tyrrell. He may have been a consistent and meticulous driver but he failed to set the world alight and retired in 1983. He returned to the cockpit for the Porsche Supercup in 1994 and he won the French GT Championship in 1998 and 1999. He has also worked as a stunt driver for the film industry.

Above: *Tyrrell-Ford driver Jean-Pierre Jarier in action during the Spanish Formula One Grand Prix*

Left: *Jean-Pierre Jarier*

Name: Jean-Pierre JARIER
Nationality: French
Born: 10th July 1946
Seasons: 1971, 1973-1983
Team/manufacturer(s): March, Shadow, Penske, Ligier, ATS, Lotus, Tyrrell, Osella
Grand Prix: 143
Race wins: 0
Championship wins: 0

Johansson

Below: *Stefan Johansson of Sweden in action in his McLaren TAG*

Stefan Johansson's father was a keen racing driver, so it was no surprise that the youngster began his karting career at the age of eight. In 1973 he won the Swedish title and moved up to Formula Ford. He won another domestic crown in 1977 before coming to the UK to take the Formula Three championship in 1980.

Johansson made his Formula One debut the same year with Shadow but he didn't qualify for either the Argentinean or Brazilian GPs and he wouldn't return to Formula One until 1983. His first points came after a solid drive at Monza in 1984, and moves to Ferrari and then McLaren brought moderate success and eight podiums.

In 1992 he retired from F1 to concentrate on Le Mans and CART racing, notching two wins in the former and being voted Rookie of the Year in the latter in 1992. He then became a team manager.

Name: Stefan Nils Edwin JOHANSSON
Nationality: Swedish
Born: 8th September 1956
Seasons: 1980, 1983-1991
Team/manufacturer(s): Shadow, Spirit, Tyrrell, Toleman, Ferrari, McLaren, Ligier, Onyx, AGS, Arrows
Grand Prix: 103
Race wins: 0
Championship wins: 0

Jones

The son of a racing driver, Alan Jones raced a Mini as a teenager before coming to England in 1967 to further his career. He was offered a drive in Formula Three in 1974 and graduated to Formula Atlantic the following year.

Jones then moved to Formula One, driving a Hesketh and then joining Graham Hill's fledgling team. His aggressive driving style took him to his first race win in Austria in 1977. A move to Williams the following season gave him four more race wins and third place in the championship.

In 1980 Jones took the drivers' title with five wins and five more podiums, and he backed it up with another strong season in 1981, although he only finished third overall. He was lured out of retirement to drive for Arrows in 1983 and Lola in 1985/6 but he couldn't recapture the glory days and retired to concentrate on touring car racing and television commitments.

Name: Alan JONES, MBE
Nationality: Australian
Born: 2nd November 1946
Seasons: 1975-1981, 1983, 1985-1986
Team/manufacturer(s): Hesketh, Hill, Surtees, Shadow, Williams, Arrows, Lola
Grand Prix: 117
Race wins: 12
Championship wins: 1

Above: Alan Jones in action in the Formula One British Grand Prix at Brands Hatch

Kovalainen

Right: *Heikki Kovalainen crosses the finish line of the Hungaroring racetrack*

Heikki Kovalainen was born in Suomussalmi in Finland. He began racing karts aged 10 in 1991 and was runner up in the Finnish Formula A championship in 1999. The following season he was Nordic champion and he also won the Elf Masters.

Kovalainen then joined the British Formula Renault championship before moving to the World Series by Nissan, a championship he won in 2004. Later that year, Kovalainen won the Race of Champions in Paris, the first non-rally driver to do so. He was promptly signed up to the GP2 Series in 2005 and finished in second place.

This led to test for Renault F1 in 2005/6, and when Fernando Alonso moved to McLaren for the 2007 season, Kovalainen was offered the race seat. He scored 11 points finishes – including a second place in Japan – and ended the championship in seventh. He then moved to McLaren and supported Lewis Hamilton in the latter's championship year. He won in Hungary and finished on the podium twice more, in Malaysia and Italy. He finished the championship in seventh place on 53 points.

The following season was much tougher, however, and he only came 12th overall. A move to Lotus and then Caterham yielded no more points finishes.

Name: Heikki KOVALAINEN
Nationality: Finnish
Born: 19th October 1981
Seasons: 2007-
Team/manufacturer(s): Renault, McLaren, Lotus, Caterham
Grand Prix: 110
Race wins: 1
Championship wins: 0

Laffite

Jacques Laffite was born in Paris during the war. He began his motorsport career as a mechanic but he didn't race seriously until he was in his late twenties. By 1972, however, he had won the French Formula Renault Championship. He moved to Formula Three the following season and took the French title.

In 1974, while racing in Formula Two, he was given a F1 drive by Frank Williams from the German GP to the end of the season. He stayed with the team in 1975 and finished a creditable second in Germany before signing for Ligier until 1982. He managed six wins and 25 podiums for the team and finished fourth in the world championship three times, in 1979, 1980 and 1981.

A move back to Williams for 1983 and 1984 was less successful and Laffite re-signed for Ligier for his last two years in Formula One. A bad crash at Brands Hatch in 1986 effectively ended his career, although he continued to race touring cars and commentated on Formula One for French television.

Name: Jacques Henri LAFFITE
Nationality: French
Born: 21st November 1943
Seasons: 1974-1986
Team/manufacturer(s): Iso Marlboro, Ligier, Williams
Grand Prix: 180
Race wins: 6
Championship wins: 0

Lang

Hermann Lang was another pre-war driver who would surely have become world champion had the series come into existence before 1950. He worked as a motorcycle mechanic to support the family after his father died and had soon saved enough to buy his own bike. He won the first race he entered and by the age of 22 was German sidecar champion.

He was offered a drive with Mercedes alongside Caracciola and proved his ability on high-speed tracks by winning the super-fast Tripoli GP three years running. In the last year before the war he recorded another four wins and took the European Championship (then motor-racing's Holy Grail).

The war undoubtedly robbed the genius of his greatest years but he returned to sportscar racing in 1949 before moving to Formula Two and eventually the new Formula One. At 45, however, he was too old to make much of an impact and he retired from racing in 1954

Name: Hermann LANG
Nationality: German
Born: 6th April 1909
Died: 19th October 1987
Seasons: 1953-1954
Team/manufacturer(s): Mercedes
Grand Prix: 2
Race wins: 0
Championship wins: 0

Lauda

Niki Lauda was born to wealthy parents in Vienna, and the family strongly discouraged his racing career in case it brought shame on the Lauda name. He spent his early teens driving around fields in an old Volkswagen Beetle, and his first race was a hill-climb in a Cooper.

With the family still refusing to back him, Lauda borrowed money and bought his way into Formula Three and then March Formula Two. By 1971 he'd been given a seat for the Austrian GP but he retired. He then endured a barren 1972 in an uncompetitive car.

With no qualifications and debts to repay, Lauda continued racing, his dedication and determination eventually paying off when he was signed by Ferrari in 1974. He won his first race in Spain and also took the chequered flag at the Dutch GP. He backed up these results with several podiums and finished fourth in the championship despite suffering mechanical problems towards the end of the season.

In 1975, Lauda dominated the championship with five wins and three more podiums. He was the favourite to take a second title the following year when he crashed inexplicably – some claim the rear suspension failed – at the German Grand Prix at the Nürburgring, a race he'd tried to boycott over track safety. The car burst into flames, trapping Lauda in the cockpit. He suffered third-degree burns, scorched lungs and several broken bones, and the last rites were given twice at his hospital bedside.

The courageous Austrian defied the odds and made a miraculous recovery. Just six weeks later, he took his place at the Italian Grand Prix. With blood seeping

Above: *Niki Lauda in action during the Formula One Monaco Grand Prix*

from the bandages on his head, he drove to an unexpected fourth place but James Hunt had now wiped out his championship lead. The title would be decided at a rain-lashed Japanese GP. Lauda understandably refused to drive in the appalling conditions and effectively surrendered the title to Hunt, but he proved himself a true champion by returning in 1977 and taking his second drivers' title.

Lauda left Ferrari for Brabham and finished fourth in the 1978 championship. The following year he struggled in an uncompetitive car and retired. He used the time to start his own airline, Lauda Air, but returned to racing with McLaren to raise more money for the business. Despite a couple of wins in 1982 the old magic seemed to have deserted him. However, by 1984 he was back

to his blistering best and he won the championship for the third time ahead of team-mate Alain Prost. Lauda retired after a poor 1985 season.

His airline was bought by the national carrier in 1999 so he took control of the Jaguar Formula One team in 2001 and 2002. In 2003, Lauda founded a low-cost airline called Niki.

Name: Andreas Nikolaus (Niki) LAUDA
Nationality: Austrian
Born: 22nd February 1949
Seasons: 1971-1979, 1982-1985
Team/manufacturer(s): March, BRM, Ferrari, Brabham, McLaren
Grand Prix: 172
Race wins: 25
Championship wins: 3

Mansell

Nigel Mansell acquired his first kart licence at the age of 10 and won his first race when he was 14. He the paid for a day in a Formula Ford and by 1977 he'd taken the series title, despite breaking his neck in a testing accident. Ignoring his doctor's advice to quit racing, Mansell signed himself out of hospital and set about working his way into F1.

He sold his house to fund a Formula Three season, and second place in the 1978 championship brought him to the attention of Lotus who offered him a drive in 1980. Mansell spent four years with the team but the cars didn't perform and he only managed five podium finishes. Frank Williams had noticed his courage and determination, however, and signed him in 1985.

Mansell now had a competitive car and he won at Brands Hatch and again in South Africa. The following season, he performed even better, recording five wins and four podiums. He would surely have taken the drivers' title had he not suffered a spectacular blow-out at 200mph in Australia that handed the championship to Alain Prost.

Despite winning six races in 1987, Mansell again missed out on the title when injuries sustained in a qualifying accident caused him to miss the last race of the season in Japan. This time the benefactor was archrival Nelson Piquet.

After a disappointing 1988, in which he retired from 12 races, Mansell joined Ferrari. He won in Brazil and Hungary and finished fourth in the championship, but, despite his huge popularity with the Italian fans, the cars were unreliable and he returned to Williams for the 1991 season. Had he not retired from the first

Above: *Nigel Mansell of Great Britain holds the trophy aloft after winning the San Marino Grand Prix*

Above: *Nigel Mansell during the Formula One Belgian Grand Prix*

three races he might have finished better than second overall, but he finally won the F1 drivers' championship in 1992 after five consecutive wins from the start of the season.

Mansell then moved across the pond to race in the CART championship. He promptly won the title, making him the only driver in history to hold both the Formula One World Championship and CART championships at the same time.

Mansell briefly returned to Williams in 1994 and won the last race of the season in Adelaide. He signed for McLaren in 1995 but wasn't comfortable in the car and

retired after just two races. He returned to touring car racing in 1998 and won the Grand Prix Masters race in Kyalami in 2005.

Name: Nigel Ernest James MANSELL, OBE
Nationality: British
Born: 8th August 1953
Seasons: 1980–1995
Team/manufacturer(s): Lotus, Williams, Ferrari, McLaren
Grand Prix: 187
Race wins: 31
Championship wins: 1

Mass

Munich-born Jochen Mass began his career in sprints and hill-climbs before moving to touring cars and winning the European Championship in 1972 in a Ford Capri. He had spells in Formula Three and Formula Two, and was offered a Formula One drive with Surtees for the latter half of the 1973 season.

The following year he moved to McLaren for the last two races but it wasn't until the Spanish Grand Prix in 1975 that he recorded his only F1 win. The race was cut short after Rolf Stommelen's Hill had crashed into a spectator area, killing five people, so only half points were awarded. Italian Lella Lombardi was running sixth at the time so she became the first, and so far only, woman to score points in Formula One.

Mass stayed with McLaren in 1976 and 1977 but the years were relatively lean and he moved to ATS, then Arrows and March in a bid to revive his fortunes. He retired from Formula One after his part in the death of Gilles Villeneuve (it was his car the Canadian struck during qualifying for the Belgian GP at Zolder) and after another big accident with Mauro Baldi at Paul Ricard.

Mass enjoyed great success in sportscars, winning the Spa 12 Hours in 1987 and Le Mans in 1989 for Mercedes.

Above: Jochen Mass in action during the Formula One British Grand Prix at Silverstone

Name: Jochen MASS
Nationality: German
Born: 30th September 1946
Seasons: 1973-1980, 1982
Team/manufacturer(s): Surtees, McLaren, ATS, Arrows, March Engineering
Grand Prix: 138
Race wins: 1
Championship wins: 0

Massa

Right: *Felipe Massa celebrates on the podium of the Magny-Cours racetrack*

When Felipe Massa delivered pizzas to the Brazilian GP aged seven, he was immediately hooked on motorsport. A year later he was racing karts and building a reputation as a driver of considerable talent.

By the time Massa was 17 he had progressed to Formula Chevrolet and he won the championship in his second season. Then, in 2000, he came to Europe and won both the Italian and the European Formula Renault Championships. The following season he won the Formula 3000 Euroseries.

He was then offered a Formula One drive with Sauber but he missed the US Grand Prix after being given a penalty in Italy. Sauber replaced him with Heinz-Harald Frentzen so he joined Ferrari as a test driver before returning to Sauber for the next two years. He drove consistently if not spectacularly and was signed by Ferrari in 2006.

He had a solid season and finished all

but two races in the top ten. He recorded his first win in Turkey and his second at his home race at the end of the season. His tally of 80 points gave him third in the drivers' standings. He performed equally well in 2007, winning another three races and taking seven podiums, although he

only finished fourth overall.

In 2008 his duel with Lewis Hamilton made for compelling viewing but the Briton just edged him out by virtue of passing Timo Glock on the last corner of the last race of the season. This was a bitter blow for Massa who, having won his home grand prix, believed that he had also secured the title. Instead, he fought back tears on the podium and took second place in the championship.

The start to the 2009 season was far from easy and Massa had hardly made an impact on the championship when a piece of Rubens Barrichello's suspension broke off the Brawn and struck him in the head. Massa's skull was fractured and he missed the rest of the season. Lesser men might have called it a day but Massa

bounced back and was on the podium for the first two races in 2010, but he wasn't as competitive for the remaining races and his title aspirations faded. 2011 and 2012 saw him score some notable finishes but he was well down the field at the end of each year and only managed two podiums, one of which was at his home grand prix.

Name: Felipe MASSA
Nationality: Brazilian
Born: 25th April 1981
Seasons: 2002, 2004-
Team/manufacturer(s): Sauber, Ferrari
Grand Prix: 174
Race wins: 11
Championship wins: 0

McLaren

Right: *The young New Zealander who gave his name to the grand prix team, Bruce McLaren*

Bruce McLaren was born in Auckland to garage owners. He studied engineering and raced an Austin Seven and Cooper-Climax in his spare time. In 1958, he finished second in the New Zealand Formula Two Championship. McLaren moved to Europe later that year and earned a drive with the Cooper Formula One team the following season. He made a good start, finishing fifth in his first Grand Prix at Monaco and winning in the USA.

He won two more races for Cooper but decided to form his own team in 1966. The outfit struggled initially but McLaren won the 1968 Belgian GP and came fifth in the championship. The following year he took third in the drivers' standings after scoring eight points finishes.

In 1970 McLaren was one of the favourites for the title but disaster struck during CanAm testing at Goodwood when his engine cover broke off and destabilised the car. McLaren was killed when the car left the track and collided with a concrete bunker, but his name lives on in one of the most successful teams of the modern era.

Name: Bruce Leslie MCLAREN
Nationality: New Zealander
Born: 30th August 1937
Died: 2nd June 1970
Seasons: 1959-1970
Team/manufacturer(s): Cooper, Eagle, McLaren
Grand Prix: 104
Race wins: 4
Championship wins: 0

Montoya

Juan Pablo Montoya began racing karts aged six. Three years later, he was the Children's National Kart Champion in Colombia. He was also the Junior Champion in 1990 and 1991.

A move to Europe in the mid-1990s saw Montoya compete in Formula Vauxhall and Formula Three, but he appeared to be sliding into obscurity until he was offered a drive in Formula 3000. He finished the season in second place and was promptly signed by Williams as a test driver in 1998. He was able to continue his Formula 3000 career, however, and won that year's title.

In 1999, Williams swapped Montoya for CART driver Alessandro Zanardi, so the Colombian found himself in the USA. He responded to the challenge and won the CART Championship at his first attempt. He backed it up by winning the Indy 500 the following year.

Montoya returned to Williams in 2001 but, despite several early-season retirements, he eventually repaid the faith by winning the Italian Grand Prix. He didn't manage another race win in 2002 but consistent points scoring saw him finish third in the championship, a position he matched by winning in Monaco and at Hockenheim in 2003.

He stayed with Williams for 2004 but only managed one win in Brazil so he moved to McLaren for 2005. He had a good season and won another three races (Britain, Italy and Brazil), which gave him fourth in the championship. He retired from Formula One partway through the 2006 season so he could concentrate on his NASCAR career.

Above: *Montoya in a Williams at the 2004 US Grand Prix at the Indianapolis Motor Speedway*

Name: Juan Pablo MONTOYA
Nationality: Colombian
Born: 20th September 1975
Seasons: 2001–2006
Team/manufacturer(s): Williams, McLaren
Grand Prix: 95
Race wins: 7
Championship wins: 0

Moss

Born in London in 1929 to Alfred, a regular at Brooklands who also raced in the 1924 Indianapolis 500, and Aileen, a keen rally driver, Stirling Moss raced an old Austin Seven around local fields from the age of nine.

His parents wanted him to become a dentist rather than a racing driver, but poor academic results saw him working in a hotel, although his interest in cars never waned and he ordered an Aspen-engined car without telling his parents. His father cancelled the order but eventually allowed Stirling to use his BMW in a series of speed trials.

Moss showed exceptional talent and immediately bought a Cooper 500 for hill-climbing and racing. He was a regular winner on the circuit and by 1950 he'd been offered a drive with the HWM Formula Two team. The following year, he was supposed to sign for Ferrari, but the team reneged on the contract. Moss was devastated and vowed revenge on the Italian team.

He didn't make an impact in Formula One until 1954. In a Maserati 250F, Moss came third in Belgium and showed enough promise in the remaining races for Mercedes to sign him for the following season. His team-mate was Juan Manuel Fangio, but Moss was not about to play second fiddle to the great Argentinean and won the British Grand Prix. Fangio took the title, however, with Moss runner up.

With two more wins and the same number of podiums, he also finished second in the 1956 championship. Moss then signed for Vanwall so that he could be with a British team, but, despite winning seven more races, he still couldn't claim the greatest prize in motorsport. He would have won

the championship in 1958 when rival Mike Hawthorn was disqualified in Portugal but Moss came to his defence and surrendered the championship by a single point.

In another underpowered British car, Moss stormed to victory at the 1961 Monaco Grand Prix, a feat he repeated at the German Grand Prix later in the year. In 1962, Moss crashed heavily at Goodwood and was in a coma for a month. Despite making a full recovery, he retired from Formula One.

Although ill fortune and his own sense of fair play conspired to deny him a world title, Moss is still rated as one of the greatest motor-racing drivers. In the first part of his career (from 1948 until his accident), he competed at 529 events.

It is a testament to his skill and courage that of these he won 212, including perhaps the greatest road race of them all, the 1955 Mille Miglia, which he and navigator Denis Jenkinson took at an average speed of 100mph. He continued racing in various forms of motorsport until 2011, a career lasting 63 years with countless triumphs.

Name: Sir Stirling MOSS, OBE
Nationality: British
Born: 17th September 1929
Seasons: 1950-1962
Team/manufacturer(s): Mercedes-Benz, Maserati, Vanwall, Cooper, Lotus
Grand Prix: 66
Race wins: 15
Championship wins: 0

Nazzaro

Felice Nazzaro was born in Turin. His rise to fame was meteoric and he won a famous triple for Fiat in 1907 (the Targa Florio in Sicily, Kaiserpreis in Germany and French GP at Dieppe). With several more victories for Fiat under his belt, Nazzaro founded his own team and promptly won the 1913 Targa Florio and the 1914 Florio Cup.

He won the French GP for the last time in Strasbourg in 1922, but then lost the European race after an oil pipe burst on the last lap. He drove his last race in 1924 but remained on the Fiat payroll until shortly before his death in 1940.

Name: Felice NAZZARO
Nationality: Italian
Born: 4th December 1881
Died: 21st March 1940
Seasons: 1907–1924
Team/manufacturer(s): Fiat, Nazzaro
Race wins: 2
Championship wins: 0

Nilsson

Gunnar Nilsson began racing in his late teens before moving to England in 1974. He joined Formula Super Vee before graduating to Formula Three, where he took the British championship with March.

In 1976, Nilsson moved to Lotus alongside Mario Andretti. In his first Formula One season Nilsson collected 11 points, including two podium finishes. The following year he won the Belgian Grand Prix in the Lotus 78 ground-effect car and finished with 20 points and eighth place in the drivers' standings.

Touted as a future F1 champion, Nilsson was diagnosed with testicular cancer and died before he could fulfil his promise. The Gunnar Nilsson Cancer Foundation was set up in his memory.

Name: Gunnar NILSSON
Nationality: Swedish
Born: 20th November 1948
Died: 20th October 1978
Seasons: 1976-1977
Team/manufacturer(s): Lotus
Grand Prix: 32
Race wins: 1
Championship wins: 0

Nuvolari

Right: *Tazio Nuvolari*

Nuvolari is another candidate for the world's finest driver honours, although he came to motor-racing late and only started riding bikes aged 27. In 1925 he won the 350cc championship and scored several more wins over the next five years in cars and on motorcycles. In 1930 he signed for Alfa Romeo and drove one of the greatest races in history at the Mille Miglia when he trailed rival Achille Varzi in the dark with his headlights off so Varzi wouldn't know he was there. The cars hit peak speeds approaching 100mph so the racing world knew they were welcoming a man with enormous talent and courage, and one who pioneered four-wheel drifting through tight corners. A few miles from the finish, Nuvolari turned on his lights and overtook a shocked Varzi just outside Brescia.

His 1931 season was plagued with mechanical problems but he still won the Italian GP, the Targa Florio and the Coppa Ciano. In 1932 he took the drivers' title after scintillating wins in Italy and France and a second place in Germany. The following season saw yet another remarkable drive in which he broke the Le Mans lap record nine times on his way to victory with Raymond Sommer.

He broke a leg in Alessandria when he swerved to avoid a stricken car but drove to fifth place in the AVUS-Rennen GP with his leg in plaster just four weeks later. By 1935 the incomparable genius was at his peak. Having failed to get a drive with Auto Union, Mercedes and Ferrari, he took on the bigger teams in an

underpowered Alfa at the German Grand Prix. Despite only having 265bhp to the five 375bhp Mercedes of Caracciola, Fagioli, Lang, von Brauchitsch and Geyer, and the four 370bhp Auto Unions of Rosemeyer, Varzi, Stuck and Pietsch, Nuvolari was inspired and trounced the opposition in what has since been called the greatest drive in GP history. Race fans were delighted but the Germans were less than impressed, especially when he repeated the feat in Barcelona and Budapest the following year.

He signed for Auto Union in 1938 and won three more GPs. Although he never formally retired from racing, his career wound down after the war and he died from a stroke in 1953. At least fifty thousand people paid their respects at his funeral.

Name: Tazio NUVOLARI
Nationality: Italian
Born: 16th November 1892
Died: 11th August 1953
Seasons: 1920-1950
Team/manufacturer(s): Alfa Romeo, Ferrari, Maserati, Auto Union
Race wins: 8
Championship wins: 1

Panis

Right: *Oliver Panis*

Olivier Panis began racing karts as a youngster before joining Pilote Elf and Formula Renault. He moved to Formula Three in 1990 and finished second in the championship the following year. Panis then moved to Formula 3000. He won a second championship in 1993 and earned a place on the Ligier Formula One team for 1994. He showed early promise, finishing second at the German GP and scoring nine points overall.

Panis picked up 16 points in 1995 and 13 in 1996, with a win at Monaco the highlight of the latter season. He moved to Prost in 1997 but missed most of the season after breaking a leg at the Canadian Grand Prix. In 1998 he wasn't as consistent and couldn't score any points.

He then took a break from Formula One before returning to drive for BAR in 2001 and 2002, and Toyota in 2003 and 2004. He remained with the Japanese team as a test driver before retiring in 2006.

Name: Olivier PANIS
Nationality: French
Born: 2nd September 1966
Seasons: 1994-1999, 2001-2004
Team/manufacturer(s): Ligier, Prost, BAR, Toyota
Grand Prix: 158
Race wins: 1
Championship wins: 0

Patrese

Riccardo Patrese hit the headlines when he won the 1974 World Karting Championship. He then won the European Formula Three Championship in 1976. The following year Patrese moved to Formula Two but he joined the Shadow Formula One team in time for the Monaco GP. He scored his first point with a sixth place finish in Japan.

He spent the next four seasons with Arrows but only managed three podium finishes. A move to Brabham in 1982 saw his luck change, however, and he won in Monaco and then again at the 1983 South African GP.

After a couple of barren years with Alfa Romeo, Patrese returned to Brabham and then signed for Williams. With a fast and reliable car underneath him, he finished third in the 1989 and 1991 drivers' standings, and nine podium finishes saw him end the season as runner-up to Nigel Mansell in Williams's all-conquering 1992 campaign. A final move to Benetton brought him fifth place in the 1993 championship.

By the end of his F1 career he'd amassed a record 256 GP starts, although several drivers have now surpassed him. Patrese returned to racing in the 2005 Grand Prix Masters series.

Name: Riccardo PATRESE
Nationality: Italian
Born: 17th April 1954
Seasons: 1977–1993
Team/manufacturer(s): Shadow, Arrows, Brabham, Alfa Romeo, Williams, Benetton
Grand Prix: 256
Race wins: 6
Championship wins: 0

Peterson

Right: *Ronnie Peterson*

Ronnie Peterson began karting as a youngster and he became Swedish champion in his late teens. He moved to Formula Three and then Formula Two, winning the European title in 1971. At the same time, he entered several Formula One races, including the 1970 Monaco Grand Prix, where he finished seventh in a March.

The following year, he finished on the podium five times and came second in the championship, which brought him to the attention of Colin Chapman and he signed for Lotus in 1973. Several early retirements undoubtedly cost him the title because a strong finish (four wins and two second places) saw him end up third overall.

In 1974, Peterson continued his good form and won the French, Italian and Monaco Grands Prix, but the Lotus 76 wasn't as competitive in 1975 and he only scored six points throughout the season.

Moves back to March for 1976 and Tyrrell for 1977 yielded a solitary win in Monza so Peterson re-signed for Lotus in 1978 and promptly won the South African and Austrian GPs. He was on course for the drivers' title when the teams headed for Monza but there was a huge crash before the first corner and Peterson was badly injured. He was taken to hospital where his condition was not thought to be life-threatening but he died from complications after surgery the following day.

Name: Bengt Ronnie PETERSON
Nationality: Swedish
Born: 14th February 1944
Died: 11th September 1978
Seasons: 1970-1978
Team/manufacturer(s): March, Tyrrell, Lotus
Grand Prix: 123
Race wins: 10
Championship wins: 0

Pironi

Didier Pironi was a talented athlete and swimmer in his youth and he also earned his pilot's licence. After a spell racing motorcycles, Pironi switched to cars and was Formula Renault Champion in 1974 and Super Renault champion the following year.

A brief stint in Formula Two led to a drive with the Tyrrell Formula One team. He finished on the podium twice before being recruited by Ligier in 1980. He looked to be capable of challenging for the drivers' title but a number of retirements in the second half of the season saw his dreams fade, although he did win the Belgian Grand Prix.

Pironi moved to Ferrari but his first season was poor and he could only manage nine points and 13th place in the championship. With wins in San Marino and Holland, and vital points in five more races, he was on course for the 1982 championship when he crashed badly before the German Grand Prix at Hockenheim. Pironi's legs were severely injured and Professor Sid Watkins briefly considered amputating them to free him from the wrecked Ferrari. He didn't race again that season and Keke Rosberg overhauled him to take the title.

By 1986, he had fully recovered but no team was willing to offer him a seat so he turned his attention to powerboat racing. His boat struck the wake of an oil tanker and flipped off the Isle of Wight in 1987. Pironi and his two crewmen were killed.

Name: Didier PIRONI
Nationality: Italian
Born: 26th March 1952
Died: 23rd August 1987
Seasons: 1978-1982
Team/manufacturer(s): Tyrrell, Ligier, Ferrari
Grand Prix: 72
Race wins: 3
Championship wins: 0

Piquet

Right: *Brazilian Nelson Piquet before the European Grand Prix at Brands Hatch*

Nelson Piquet was the son of a government minister and had a privileged upbringing. He was a talented tennis player and was sent to sports school in San Francisco, but, to the disappointment of his parents, he became more interested in motor-racing.

He began entering karting championships and established himself as a competent driver who would win the Brazilian Championship in his second year. His father insisted he return to the USA to finish his engineering course but Piquet continued racing and won the 1976 Brazilian SuperVee Championship.

Piquet moved to European Formula Three in 1977 and finished third in the championship, a title he then won the following season. These noteworthy performances led to a F1 drive with Brabham alongside Niki Lauda. After a promising first season, Piquet was promoted to team leader and won his first race at Long Beach. Two more wins and

three podiums saw him challenge Alan Jones for the 1980 drivers' title but the Australian edged him out.

Another three wins and four podiums gave Piquet the championship in 1981 but, despite a single win in Canada in 1982, he was off the pace. He was back on form in 1983, however. Wins at the Brazilian, Italian and European GPs, and solid performances throughout the season, gave him a second drivers' title.

The next two years were less successful, partly because Brabham was experimenting with a new turbocharged BMW engine. He won in Canada, Detroit and France but was otherwise frustrated by mechanical problems and moved to Williams in 1986. Four wins

and six podiums in his first year should have been enough to take the title for a third time but Alain Prost and Nigel Mansell squeezed him into third.

Piquet roared back in 1987 in a golden era for the sport. Together with compatriot Ayrton Senna, their epic duels with Mansell and Prost have entered F1 folklore. Despite winning fewer races than the Englishman, he scored consistently throughout the season and took his third title by 12 points.

He then signed for Lotus for a huge salary but the move was ill-advised and he moved again, to Benetton, in 1990. He managed two wins in his first year and one more in 1991 but no team was prepared to meet his wage demands in 1992 so he moved to the USA instead. He was injured in practice for the Indianapolis 500 and promptly retired back to Brazil.

Piquet pursued a number of business interests and continued to compete in sportscar racing. He also managed son Nelson Junior's early racing career.

Above Nelson Piquet of Brazil as he enters the tunnel in his Lotus Judd during the Monaco Grand Prix

Name: Nelson PIQUET
Nationality: Brazilian
Born: 17th August 1952
Seasons: 1978-1991
Teams: Ensign, Brabham, Williams, Lotus, Benetton
Grand Prix: 207
Race wins: 23
Championship wins: 3

Prost

Below: *Alain Prost*

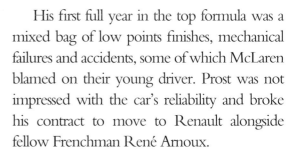

Alain Marie Pascal Prost was born near St-Étienne, France, in February 1955. Young Alain was always destined to be short but his height didn't stop him developing into a footballer of considerable talent. Having tried karting at the age of 14, however, Prost hung up his boots and devoted his attention to motorsport.

He soon showed his talent for karting by winning several championships, and he left school in 1974 to pursue the sport full-time. He won the 1975 Senior French Championship and earned a place in Formula Renault as a result. He won this series twice and the French and European Formula 3 titles in 1979. By now he was hot property and several Formula 1 teams tried to secure his signature. McLaren offered him a drive in the last race of the 1979 season at Watkins Glen, but he surprised everyone and turned it down because he knew he wasn't fully prepared. He valued their offer so highly, however, that he signed for the 1980 season anyway.

His first full year in the top formula was a mixed bag of low points finishes, mechanical failures and accidents, some of which McLaren blamed on their young driver. Prost was not impressed with the car's reliability and broke his contract to move to Renault alongside fellow Frenchman René Arnoux.

Although the all-French team looked perfect on paper, Arnoux was immediately wary of his supremely talented team-mate and couldn't stop the young driver winning three races, including his first at his home grand prix. Prost went on to finish fifth in the championship just seven points behind world champion Nelson Piquet.

The following year Prost won two more races and came fourth in the championship, but his relationship with Arnoux and the French press had reached rock bottom. Something had to give, and it was Arnoux who left the team. Prost promptly won four races in the 1983 season and only missed out on the overall championship because he felt the team had been too conservative towards the end of the season. Renault disagreed and fired him immediately. Prost was promptly re-hired by a resurgent McLaren.

Although Senna's star was on the rise, Prost was now with the best team and driving one of the best cars and he dominated the 1984 season, winning seven races and only losing out on the overall championship to team-mate Niki Lauda by a half point (half points were awarded for the black-flagged Monaco Grand Prix that Senna nearly won). The following year, 1985, Prost won five more races and became the first French World Champion.

Despite being behind on points before the last race of the 1986 season in Australia, championship favourite Nigel Mansell had a high-speed blow-out and team-mate Nelson Piquet pitted for new tyres as a precaution. Prost drove a problem-free race and successfully defended his title. In 1987 he overtook Jackie Stewart's record of 27 F1 victories, but his car was a little off the pace and he finished the season in fourth place.

In 1988 the McLaren pair of Prost and Senna blew the other teams away. Although Prost outscored Senna, only a driver's best 11 results counted and Senna took the title. Their intense rivalry finally came to a head at the 1989 Japanese Grand Prix. Prost knew that if neither driver finished he would win the championship on points. The two McLarens collided at the chicane and Prost retired, but Senna continued after being given an illegal push-start by the marshals. He was eventually disqualified and Prost clinched the championship.

The 1990 championship was eerily familiar, only this time Senna would be

champion if either driver failed to finish in Japan. Senna left nothing to chance and deliberately drove into Prost's Ferrari as they turned in for the first corner. It was a reckless move that somehow went unpunished. Prost stayed with Ferrari but he was sacked for criticising the team at the end of a poor 1991 campaign.

There was no time to sign for another team before the 1992 season so he took a sabbatical and joined Williams in 1993. He won seven races and took the championship for a fourth time. Despite this, Williams dropped Prost in favour of Ayrton Senna for 1994 so the Frenchman retired with a then-record 51 wins.

He worked as a commentator for French television as well as a consultant for Renault and McLaren. In 1997 he bought the Ligier team and renamed it Prost Grand Prix but the venture was short-lived and he now works as an ambassador for Renault.

Above: *Alain Prost of France holds the trophy aloft after his victory in the Brazilian Grand Prix*

Name: Alain Marie Pascal PROST, OBE
Nationality: French
Born: 24th February 1955
Seasons: 1980-1991, 1993
Teams: McLaren, Renault, Ferrari, Williams
Grand Prix: 202
Race wins: 51
Championship wins: 4

Räikkönen

Kimi Räikkönen began racing karts aged 10. His talent was immediately obvious and he moved to the UK to join the British Formula Renault Winter series in 1999. He then won the Formula Renault Championship the following year.

Räikkönen was signed by the Sauber Formula One team for the 2001 season but a number of retirements ruined what would have been a respectable debut year. He moved to McLaren but was again let down by his machine, although he still finished sixth in the championship. In 2003, his car was competitive and he won the Malaysian Grand Prix. Nine more podiums saw him finish second in the championship behind Michael Schumacher.

The 2004 season wasn't as successful and he only registered one win, but he fought back in 2005, notching seven wins and five podiums to end the year in second place. The 2006 campaign was tougher and he only finished fifth overall.

After Michael Schumacher's retirement, Räikkönen moved from McLaren to Ferrari in a deal reportedly worth £35 million per year. It would be an eventful season as he battled for the championship with Lewis Hamilton and Fernando Alonso. He scored consistently throughout the year and rattled up six wins to the McLaren pair's four each, but he was still behind going into the last race in Brazil and needed a miracle. Hamilton drove poorly and Alonso couldn't live with his searing pace so he took the title by a point.

Räikkönen won two of the first four races in 2008 but faded to finish third in Hamilton's championship year. After a poor 2009 he announced his retirement from the sport. Having seen Schumacher return, however, Räikkönen made a comeback in 2012 with Lotus. The season started slowly but he then scored consistently and was in contention for the title until the last few races. He made an encouraging start to the 2013 season with a win in Melbourne.

Name: Kimi Matias RÄIKKÖNEN
Nationality: Finnish
Born: 17th October 1979
Seasons: 2001-2009, 2012-
Team/manufacturer(s): Sauber, McLaren, Ferrari, Lotus
Grand Prix: 178
Race wins: 20
Championship wins: 1

Regazzoni

Born Gianclaudio, but better known as Clay, Regazzoni began racing a De Tomaso in the early 1960s at the comparatively late age of 24. By 1970 he had won the European Formula Two Championship. Regazzoni joined Ferrari for the latter part of the same season and made an immediate impression by winning in Italy and finishing third in the championship.

The next two years saw Regazzoni retire from strong positions and he could only finish seventh in the championship. He moved to BRM for 1973 but didn't taste success until he re-signed for Ferrari in 1974. He ended the season second in the championship behind Emerson Fittipaldi but the following two years brought only two more wins.

Regazzoni moved to Ensign in 1977 and Shadow in 1978 but the cars were not competitive and he didn't win again until racing for Williams at the 1979 British GP. He began the 1980 season with Ensign but crashed at the US West Grand Prix and was paralyzed from the waist down.

Regazzoni actively encouraged disabled people to race and helped develop hand-control systems for their cars. He died in a road accident in Italy in 2006.

Name: Gianclaudio Giuseppe (Clay) REGAZZONI
Nationality: Swiss
Born: 5th September 1939
Died: 15th December 2006
Seasons: 1970-1980
Team/manufacturer(s): Ferrari, BRM, Ensign, Shadow, Williams
Grand Prix: 132
Race wins: 5
Championship wins: 0

Above: *Clay Reggazoni at Zandvoort in 1971*

Reutemann

Carlos Reutemann raced touring cars and in Formula Two in Argentina before he moved to Europe and finished second in the 1970 F2 championship. This led to a drive with the Brabham Formula One team in 1972. Reutemann made an immediate impact by taking pole position for his first GP at his home circuit, a race in which he eventually finished seventh.

Reutemann stayed with Brabham until 1976 but his results were a mixed bag that included three race wins and six retirements in 1974, another win and five podiums in 1975 (in a season that saw him finish third in the championship), and nine retirements in 11 races in 1976.

Reutemann moved to Ferrari in 1977 and enjoyed a good season with a win in Brazil and a further five podium finishes. He finished fourth in the championship and went one better in 1978 after recording another four wins.

After a difficult year with Lotus, Reutemann joined Williams in 1980 and a win and seven podiums saw him finish the season in third overall. The following year, he launched a determined assault on the title but was pipped by Nelson Piquet.

Reutemann and Frank Williams came to blows over team politics after two races of the 1982 season and the Argentinean promptly retired from Formula One. He later entered the political arena in his home country, although he did come third at the Rally of Argentina.

Name: Carlos Alberto REUTEMANN
Nationality: Argentinean
Born: 12th April 1942
Seasons: 1972-1982
Team/manufacturer(s): Brabham, Ferrari, Lotus, Williams
Grand Prix: 146
Race wins: 12
Championship wins: 0

Revson

Peter Revson was heir to the Revlon Cosmetics empire so he enjoyed a privileged upbringing surrounded by fast cars and boats. He began making waves in events in the US in the early 1960s but soon moved to Europe to further his career. His first season in F1 was unsuccessful so he returned to the US and teamed up with Steve McQueen to finish second in a sportscar race at Sebring. He also drove in the 1971 US GP at Watkins Glen but was forced to retire. However, he started on pole for that year's Indy 500 and eventually came second.

Revson was then offered a drive with McLaren and he repaid the faith with four podium finishes, including a second place in Canada. The following year he won the British and Canadian GPs and finished fifth in the drivers' standings.

He moved to Shadow for the 1974 season but he was killed when his suspension failed during practice for the South African Grand Prix.

Name: Peter Jeffrey REVSON
Nationality: American
Born: 27th February 1939
Died: 22nd March 1974
Seasons: 1964, 1971-1974
Team/manufacturer(s): Revson, Parnell, McLaren, Shadow
Grand Prix: 33
Race wins: 2
Championship wins: 0

Above: *Peter Revson at the Nurburgring in 1973*

Rindt

After his parents were killed during an air raid in WWII, German-born Jochen Rindt moved to Austria to live with his grandparents. His career began in Formula Two and a number of successes saw him break into Formula One with a Rob Walker Brabham in 1964, although he failed to finish his home GP.

He moved to Cooper but his first year brought little success. In 1966, however, Rindt recorded three podiums and came third in the drivers' championship. A move to Brabham failed to bring results, and neither did his first year with Lotus but, in 1970, despite an inauspicious start to the season, he then won in Monaco. Later in the year he won four consecutive races in Holland, France, Britain and Germany, which gave him a big lead in the drivers' standings.

During practice for the Italian Grand Prix, Rindt decided to have the wings removed from his Lotus 72 to give him a higher top speed (so that he could compete against the more powerful Ferraris). He lost control of the car coming into the Parabolica corner and hit a poorly installed crash barrier. Rindt's car smashed into a stanchion and his seatbelt inflicted fatal injuries to his chest and throat.

Rindt's lead in the championship was not unassailable but team-mate Emerson Fittipaldi deprived Jacky Ickx of the points he needed at the last race of the season and so Rindt became the only posthumous world champion. The trophy was presented to his widow, Nina. It later emerged that Rindt had promised to retire if he won the title.

Name: Karl Jochen RINDT
Nationality: Austrian
Born: 18th April 1942
Died: 5th September 1970
Seasons: 1964-1970
Team/manufacturer(s): Brabham, Cooper, Lotus
Grand Prix: 61
Race wins: 6
Championship wins: 1

Rodríguez

Born in Mexico City, Pedro Rodríguez was a national motorcycle champion in 1953 and 1954. In 1957 he switched allegiance and joined Ferrari. He was initially lured to Europe by the glamour of Le Mans, a race he entered 14 times, although he only won once, in 1968.

Rodríguez was handed a Formula One lifeline by Lotus in 1963 (he drove in the US and Mexican GPs), but he didn't make an impact in the sport until he won in South Africa in 1967 driving for Cooper.

The following year, Rodríguez joined BRM, and, having recorded three podium finishes, came sixth in the championship. After a brief but unsuccessful stint with Ferrari, he returned to BRM and won again at the 1970 Belgian GP but poor results for the remainder of the season saw him only finish seventh overall.

Rodríguez was killed at the wheel of his Ferrari 512M when he crashed during a sportscar race in Germany in July 1971.

Above: *Rodríguez at the 1968 Dutch Grand Prix*

Name: Pedro RODRÍGUEZ
Nationality: Mexican
Born: 18th January 1940
Died: 11th July 1971
Seasons: 1963-1971
Team/manufacturer(s): Ferrari, Lotus, Cooper, BRM
Grand Prix: 54
Race wins: 2
Championship wins: 0

Rosberg

Keke Rosberg was born in Stockholm to Finnish parents. He was a three-time national kart champion before he graduated to Formula Vee and Super Vee. After a spell in Formula Two, Rosberg made his Formula One debut in 1978 with the Theodore Team at the relatively old age of 29 but he had little success in his first season and couldn't improve the following year with Wolf.

A move to Fittipaldi in 1980 brought Rosberg to the attention of the bigger teams and he eventually signed for Williams in 1982, a year that saw him score points in 10 of the 16 races and included a win at the Swiss Grand Prix. He ended the campaign on 44 points, which, in a low-scoring season, was enough to clinch the world championship.

Rosberg stayed with Williams for the next three seasons but although he won at Monaco, USA (twice) and Australia, the closest he came to winning another title was third in 1985. The following year he moved to McLaren but only managed 22 points and sixth place overall. This was his last season in Formula One as he retired at the end of a disappointing year.

In 1989, Rosberg made a comeback of sorts in the Spa 24 Hours and he also entered several sportscar events in the early 1990s. He then founded a German touring car team. His son, Nico, joined Williams in 2006 and now partners Lewis Hamilton at Mercedes.

Name: Keijo Erik 'Keke' ROSBERG
Nationality: Finnish
Born: 6th December 1948
Seasons: 1978-1986
Team/manufacturer(s): Theodore, ATS, Wolf, Fittipaldi, Williams, McLaren
Grand Prix: 114
Race wins: 5
Championship wins: 1

Rosemeyer

Bernd Rosemeyer worked on motorcycles and cars in his father's workshop, and he was soon asked to join the fledgling Auto Union team with their 500bhp silver arrows. The mid-engined cars were notoriously difficult to drive but Rosemeyer (and Nuvolari) tamed the beasts and the young German almost beat the great Caracciola at the Nürburgring in only his second race. He then won three consecutive races at the daunting track, one in thick fog.

He drove to sensational victories at the Italian, German, Swiss and Donnington GPs in 1936 – a year in which he was crowned European Champion – and in 1937 he also took the Vanderbilt Cup in the US. This fabulous driver was killed at the peak of his powers when his land-speed-record car left the road – probably due to high crosswinds – at over 270mph. Rosemeyer was thrown from the car as it went airborne and died at the roadside after hitting a bridge.

Above:
Rosemeyer tests his Auto-Union on the high-speed banking

Name: Bernd ROSEMEYER
Nationality: German
Born: 14th October 1909
Died: 28th January 1938
Team/manufacturer(s): Auto Union
Race wins: 10
Championship wins: 1

Scheckter

Right: *Jody Scheckter driving the Formula One Ferrari during the Spanish Grand Prix*

Jody Scheckter began racing karts as a boy in South Africa. He soon progressed to motorcycles and then saloon cars. After winning his domestic Formula Ford series, he travelled to Europe and drove in Formula Ford and Formula Three.

His talent was spotted by McLaren and he was offered a drive in Formula One at the age of only 22. He made his debut at the 1972 US Grand Prix at Watkins Glen and finished ninth. A poor second season yielded no points so he signed for Tyrrell in 1974 and by mid-season had recorded his first win in Sweden. He backed it up with another win at Silverstone and finished the season third overall with 45 points.

Although he registered another two wins, Scheckter couldn't challenge for the title in 1975 or 1976 so he signed for Wolf in 1977. He won three races and scored points at six more in his first year for the team but he was beaten to the title by Niki Lauda. He couldn't repeat this success in 1978 so he moved to Ferrari. Scheckter won another three races and scored points at nine more which was enough to give him the drivers' title.

His defence of the title was uncharacteristically poor so he retired from F1 and moved to the US to concentrate on a weapons simulation venture. He then returned to the UK and diversified into organic farming.

Name: Jody David SCHECKTER
Nationality: South African
Born: 29th January 1950
Seasons: 1972-1980
Team/manufacturer(s): McLaren, Tyrrell, Wolf, Ferrari
Grand Prix: 113
Race wins: 10
Championship wins: 1

Schumacher, Michael

Michael Schumacher started racing a kart his father Rolf had built when he was only five. Rolf also managed a local track so Schumacher had plenty of opportunity to perfect his driving skills. Aged 12, he began racing karts competitively and won numerous championships throughout Europe during his teens.

Schumacher graduated to Formula Ford in 1988 and then moved to German Formula Three for the next two years. He took the championship in 1990 and was offered a drive at Spa for Jordan at the 1991 Belgian GP. Schumacher qualified seventh but had to retire from the race, although he'd shown enough promise for Benetton to sign him for the rest of the season.

In 1992, he won his first Formula One race for the team, also at Spa, and he finished the season in third place after recording a further seven podiums. Another eight podiums and

a win in 1993 highlighted his talent, but he had to wait until 1994 for his first drivers' championship. He won six of the first seven races but was then disqualified at Silverstone for failing to serve a stop-go penalty. He was disqualified again for irregularities with the car's skid block at Spa. While serving a two-race ban for the first offence, Damon Hill slashed his advantage in the championship.

At the last race of the season in Australia, Schumacher and Hill collided after the German made a mistake and ran wide. Instead of letting Hill past, he appeared to steer into the Englishman, the damage putting Hill out and handing Schumacher the title by a single point. He managed to avoid controversy in 1995 and his nine race wins gave him the title by 30 points.

In 1996 Schumacher moved to Ferrari, but the team was not the force it once was and hadn't won a title since 1979. Three wins and

five podiums brought him third place in the championship, and the following year the car was a serious title challenger.

But 1997 marked a low point in Schumacher's career. Five wins and three seconds saw him vying with Jacques Villeneuve for the driver honours but history repeated itself at the European GP in Jerez when he appeared to steer into the Canadian to stop him overtaking and potentially winning the championship. This time the stewards found Schumacher guilty and disqualified him from the entire season.

Ferrari were still a team in transition but the pieces were falling into place. Schumacher won another eight GPs in 1998 and 1999, but an accident at Silverstone midway through the latter season saw him sidelined for six races. Team-mate Eddie Irvine almost took the title and helped the team to their first constructors' title for 16 years.

Over the next five seasons, Schumacher won 48 races, taking the title from 2000 until 2004. His astonishing success finally eclipsed Juan Manuel Fangio and completely rewrote the record books. In 2004, for example, he won 13 of 18 races. New tyre regulations penalised the team and he could only finish third in 2005, although he improved to second behind Fernando Alonso in 2006.

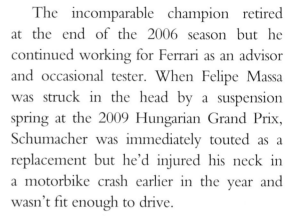

The incomparable champion retired at the end of the 2006 season but he continued working for Ferrari as an advisor and occasional tester. When Felipe Massa was struck in the head by a suspension spring at the 2009 Hungarian Grand Prix, Schumacher was immediately touted as a replacement but he'd injured his neck in a motorbike crash earlier in the year and wasn't fit enough to drive.

He spent the winter getting into shape and announced that he would be returning to Formula One with Mercedes. Despite numerous points-scoring finishes, the old magic deserted him and he only managed a single podium in the following three seasons. His reputation as the finest driver of his generation and one of the greatest of all time was never in doubt, however, and he entered permanent retirement after a glittering career at the end of the 2012 season.

Name: Michael SCHUMACHER
Nationality: German
Born: 3rd January 1969
Seasons: 1991–2006, 2010–2012
Team/manufacturer(s): Jordan, Benetton, Ferrari, Mercedes
Grand Prix: 308
Race wins: 91
Championship wins: 7

Schumacher, Ralf

As the younger brother of a seven-time world champion, Ralf was clearly going to have to work hard to gain recognition. He began racing karts at the age of three and by 1995 had finished third in the German Formula Three Championship. A year later, he won the Japanese Formula Nippon Championship.

Schumacher tested for McLaren in 1996, but ended up driving for Jordan. He had a mixed first season with several retirements, five top-six finishes and a podium in only his third GP (Argentina). The following year, he came second in Belgium and third in Italy but it was only after a move to Williams in 1999 that Schumacher came out of his brother's shadow.

He had to wait until the 2001 San Marino GP for his first win for the team, but he followed it up with victories in Canada and Germany and fourth place in the championship. He was solid if not spectacular during 2002 and 2003 and was on course for another promising year when a crash at the 2004 United States Grand Prix at Indianapolis saw him sidelined for six races.

Having joined Toyota from Williams, Schumacher's fortunes declined after a promising start and he only finished sixth in the 2005 championship. He finished on the podium once more and scored points at six events in 2006 but he was still only tenth overall. He only managed 16th place in 2007 and was not offered another drive. Despite stating that he would like to continue racing in Formula One, he switched to DTM and then rejected the advances of new teams like USF1, HRT, Virgin and Lotus in 2010.

Name: Ralf SCHUMACHER
Nationality: German
Born: 30th June 1975
Seasons: 1997-2007
Team/manufacturer(s): Jordan, Williams, Toyota
Grand Prix: 182
Race wins: 6
Championship wins: 0

Seagrave

Henry Seagrave was born to an American mother and Irish father in Baltimore. He was raised in Ireland but was schooled at Eton and served as a fighter pilot in the Royal Flying Corps during the First World War. He was recruited to the RAF in 1919 but resigned due to two injuries sustained during the conflict.

He pestered Talbot for a drive at the 1921 Brooklands 200 Miles and promptly won the race. He then won at the French GP, in Tours and at San Sebastian in a Sunbeam, becoming the first British driver to win a grand prix in a British car. After another win at Miramas, he decided to concentrate on breaking the land speed record.

In 1926, he claimed the record for Britain in a modified Sunbeam Tiger on Southport Sands with a speed of just over 150mph. He became the first person to drive at more than 200mph when he took his 1000hp Sunbeam to Daytona Beach in the US. His final record (231mph)

came at the same venue in the beautiful Golden Arrow in 1929, a feat for which he was knighted. This dashing hero of motor-racing's golden age was killed when his boat, Miss England II, struck an object and capsized on Lake Windermere while setting a new water-speed record (98.76mph).

Name: Sir Henry O'Neal de Hane SEAGRAVE
Nationality: British
Born: 22nd September 1896
Died: 13th June 1930
Seasons: 1921-1924
Team/manufacturer(s): Talbot Darracq, Sunbeam
Race wins: 5
Championship wins: 0

Seaman

Richard Seaman was born into a wealthy family who allowed him to indulge his childhood passion for racing cars. In 1934 he took an MG to Europe and won in Berne. He then bought an ERA and, having won at Pescara, Berne and Brno, restored an old Delage and humiliated top-class opposition by winning another four races and then taking the Empire Trophy in an outclassed Maserati. He was immediately asked by Alfred Neubauer to test for Mercedes at the Nürburgring. Against his family's wishes he signed for the pro-Nazi team in 1937 and placed second in the Vanderbilt Cup.

Seaman gave a Nazi salute on the podium after winning the 1938 German GP, endearing himself to Hitler in the process. He also married a German woman, Erica Popp, daughter of BMW's director. He was leading the 1939 Belgian GP at Spa when he crashed into a tree. He was knocked unconscious and died later from his burns.

Name: Richard SEAMAN
Nationality: British
Born: 4th February 1913
Died: 25th June 1939
Seasons: 1936-1939
Team/manufacturer(s): ERA, Scuderia Torino, Mercedes-Benz
Grand Prix: 23
Race wins: 6
Championship wins: 0

Above: *Richard Seaman at the wireless control of an MG car*

Senna

Right: *Ayrton Senna*

Ayrton Senna da Silva was born in São Paulo, Brazil, in March 1960. The family were wealthy business people and landowners, and his father, a motorsport enthusiast, presented the young Ayrton with a tiny lawnmower engine-powered kart when he was only four. Initially awkward and with a lack of focus, Senna suddenly found something that interested him, but Brazilian law prevented him from racing until his 13th birthday. His first race at the Interlagos kart complex was against talented local prospects, but Senna won and the legend was born.

Four years later he won the first of two South American Kart Championships, before heading to Europe for the World Championships at Le Mans, where he finished a respectable sixth against seasoned drivers with far more experience. He arrived in England in 1981 to drive for Ralph Firman's Van Diemen team in the Formula Ford Championship, and he promptly won both of the series he was contesting.

There were several Brazilian drivers looking for places in the higher formulas in the early '80s and, as Senna didn't have financial backing to help the teams, he was overlooked. He decided to retire and return to Brazil to work for his father. He immediately regretted the decision, talked his father into sponsoring him and returned to England to win 22 races and the 1982 championship. Formula Three was the next step, but Martin Brundle would provide a stern test during the 1983 season. The Englishman was one of the first to appreciate Senna's incredible skill, but he was also the first to feel the pressure Senna piled on you if you were racing him wheel to wheel: "He made you believe that he would rather have an accident than yield to you. He had this obsession to win at all costs."

Senna won the final race and took the title, which immediately caught the attention of Formula One team bosses. Brabham expressed an interest but Nelson

Above: *Ayrton Senna of Brazil in action during the F1 Hungarian Grand Prix*

Piquet blocked Senna's move, so the Brazilian took the only remaining option and joined Toleman, a second-tier team that was unlikely to help him achieve good results. His first few outings were dogged by mechanical failures and poor finishes, but he somehow managed to qualify 13th for the Monaco Grand Prix. Senna was already making a name for himself as a superb wet-weather racer and the heavens opened soon after the start.

With more experienced drivers making mistakes, Senna gradually carved his way through the field and by lap seven he was up to sixth place. He continued pushing hard and when Mansell and Lauda both span out Senna found himself in second, 34 seconds behind Alain Prost. Eleven laps later he was only seven seconds adrift, a quite remarkable drive considering the man ahead and the conditions. With the rain pouring down, Senna eventually overtook the Frenchman but the organisers stopped the race on the same lap, thus denying the young Brazilian a debut victory (the last full lap completed by all the drivers was deemed to be the end of the race).

His performances and ninth place in the world championship had piqued the interest of Lotus, however, and he signed for them the following season. Now that he had a competitive car, Senna was ready to challenge for the greatest prize in motorsport. He won the 1985 Portuguese GP, his first, in torrential rain, then backed it up with seven pole positions,

Above: *Ayrton Senna waves to the crowd after winning the German Grand Prix*

two podium finishes and a win at Spa. He finished fourth in the championship won by Prost, but his searing pole position laps hinted at the greatness to come. He also performed well in 1986 and was leading the championship until poor reliability saw him fall behind Mansell, Piquet and eventual champion Prost.

Lotus secured a deal with engine manufacturer Honda for 1987 and Senna started the season strongly. However, the Williams cars of Piquet and Mansell were too strong and he eventually finished the season in third, one place ahead of Prost. The Frenchman was so impressed with Senna's driving that he convinced McLaren team principle Ron Dennis to hire him as the number two driver for 1988. Senna had a great relationship with Honda, so McLaren got the best engine as part of the deal. All the pieces were in place and the stage was set for the most dangerous and controversial rivalry in the history of sport.

Senna took pole in the first race of the 1988 season at Interlagos, but mechanical failure forced him out and allowed Prost to take the chequered flag. McLaren also dominated at Imola with the turbo-powered cars lapping the entire field. This time Senna took the win with Prost in second. Senna out-qualified the more conservative Prost by over a second in Monaco, but Prost drove an inspired race and set the fastest lap. Senna was so determined to beat his time that he crashed into the wall before the tunnel and handed his team-mate victory. It was his lowest point so far in Formula One and he fled to an apartment in the principality to dwell on his error.

The two traded pole positions and race wins (apart from at Monza, where both McLarens retired, ruining a perfect season) before the Belgian Grand Prix at Spa. Senna had copied Prost's aerodynamic settings for all of the previous races and Prost was annoyed that the Brazilian had scored six wins to his four. So he changed his settings at the last minute. The plan backfired however, and Senna won comfortably. The title was decided at Suzuka. Senna stalled at the start and handed Prost the advantage but when it began to rain he clawed his way back into contention and took the win and the championship.

The following year, the rivalry between the pair escalated. Prost took the championship after blocking Senna at the chicane in Japan and forcing both drivers out. However, Senna had his revenge at the same circuit in 1990, although he later admitted to driving into Prost deliberately. Senna's 1991 season yielded seven wins, five more podiums and the drivers' title but he wasn't as dominant in 1992 because Mansell's Williams was the superior car. Prost took the 1993 title, also for Williams, so Senna was doubly hungry for success come 1994.

Senna failed to finish the first two races and handed the advantage to Michael Schumacher. San Marino was a make or break race for him but the weekend was marred by tragedy. Rubens Barrichello's car left the track and smashed into the catch fencing, hospitalising the Brazilian. Then, during Saturday's practice session, Austrian Roland Ratzenberger was killed when his front wing failed and he hit the wall at full speed.

Senna almost retired but he chose to race on the Sunday with an Austrian flag in his cockpit, which he planned to raise during his lap of honour. The start of the race saw Pedro Lamy's Lotus career into JJ Lehto's stalled Benetton. One

of the wheels left the track and injured nine people in the grandstand. After the restart, Senna's Williams left the track at the high-speed Tamburello corner and hit an unprotected concrete wall at around 135mph. A piece of the front suspension struck him in the head and penetrated his helmet. It also forced his head back against the headrest with such force that it fractured his skull.

Senna's death shocked the world and over three million people – the largest such gathering in modern times – lined the streets of Sao Paulo at his funeral.

Above: Ayrton Senna of Brazil in action during the F1 Belgian Grand Prix

Name: Ayrton SENNA
Nationality: Brazilian
Born: 21st March 1960
Died: 1st May 1994
Seasons: 1984-1994
Team/manufacturer(s): Toleman Hart, Lotus, McLaren Honda, Williams
Grand Prix: 162
Race wins: 41
Championship wins: 3

Siffert

Right: *Jo Siffert at Brands Hatch*

Jo Siffert began racing motorcycles after the Second World War and was Swiss 350cc champion in 1959. He then moved to Formula Junior before making the grade in Formula One, although he made little impression in his underpowered Lotus-Climax.

A move to Brabham in 1964 brought Siffert his first podium but he then endured several years of mediocrity until he won the 1968 British Grand Prix in a Lotus 49B, a year in which also won Le Mans and the Sebring 12 Hours in a Porsche. The following season he finished fifth in the championship but it wasn't until 1971 that Siffert won his next F1 race in Austria.

Towards the end of the season, he entered a non-championship event at Brands Hatch. He was killed when the suspension on his BRM – already damaged after a collision with Ronnie Peterson – failed and he crashed heavily. The car caught fire but Siffert couldn't escape the burning wreck. The accident led to a review of safety equipment, the adoption of on-board fire extinguishers, piped air to the driver and better fire-retardant overalls.

Name: Joseph (Jo) SIFFERT
Nationality: Swiss
Born: 7th July 1936
Died: 24th October 1971
Seasons: 1962-1971
Team/manufacturer(s): Lotus, Cooper, Brabham, March, BRM
Grand Prix: 100
Race wins: 2
Championship wins: 0

Sommer

Raymond Sommer was born into a wealthy family of carpet makers, and his father, Roger, broke the Wright brothers' record for the longest flight in 1909. Raymond, who acquired the nickname the 'Gay Cavalier', started racing in the early 1930s and soon developed a reputation for both his grim determination and flamboyant driving style.

He won at Le Mans in 1932 and 1933, the latter alongside the great Tazio Nuvolari, and also took the French GP in 1936. He was national champion the following year, as well as in 1939 and 1946. He gave Enzo Ferrari the team's first victory at the Turin Grand Prix before joining Talbot-Lago for the first Formula One World Championship in 1950.

He entered a minor race at Haute-Garonne in September but the steering on his Cooper failed and he was killed in the resulting crash.

Above: *Racing driver Raymond Sommer makes a point.*

Name: Raymond SOMMER
Nationality: French
Born: 31st August 1906
Died: 10th September 1950
Seasons: 1950
Team/manufacturer(s): Ferrari, Talbot-Lago
Grand Prix: 5
Race wins: 2
Championship wins: 0

Stewart

STEWART

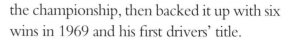

Below: *Jackie Stewart in his BRM car at the Monaco Grand Prix*

Jackie Stewart almost missed out on a career in racing because his older brother, Jimmy, who had been making a name for himself, was injured in a crash at Le Mans. Their parents decided that motor-racing was not a suitable sport so Jackie was encouraged to try target shooting. He was so good that he almost qualified for the 1960 Olympics.

Stewart couldn't resist the lure of racing, however, and he impressed Ken Tyrrell at Oulton Park in 1963. Tyrrell then asked him to test for Formula Cooper and offered him a drive in Formula Three.

Stewart won his first race for Tyrrell the following year but he was keen for a move into Formula One. Tyrrell couldn't offer him a seat so he moved to BRM and started by scoring points in seven of his first eight races – including a win at Monza – and securing third in the championship. The 1966 and '67 seasons were less productive but a move to Matra in 1968 saw him realise his potential. He won three races and finished second in the championship, then backed it up with six wins in 1969 and his first drivers' title.

By now Tyrrell had joined the F1 circus and the team persuaded Stewart to rejoin them. He suffered eight retirements in his first year back but took the title in 1971 with another six wins. Had he not been ill for the Belgian GP, he might have won again in 1972, but he was back to his best in 1973, a season in which he won five more races and took the title for the third time.

Stewart retired following the death of team-mate Francois Cevert at Watkins Glen. He championed safety in the sport and also acted as a consultant with Ford before setting up his own F1 team in 1997 with drivers of the calibre of Rubens Barrichello and Johnny Herbert. The latter came second at Monaco but the team didn't reach its potential and was taken over by Ford in 2000.

Name: Sir John Young (Jackie) STEWART, OBE
Nationality: British
Born: 11th June 1939
Seasons: 1965-1973
Team/manufacturer(s): BRM, Matra, March, Tyrrell
Grand Prix: 100
Race wins: 27
Championship wins: 3

Stuck

Hans Stuck was born in Poland to Swiss parents who lived in Germany but he is perhaps best-known as the 'Austrian King of the Mountains' because of his extraordinary record in hill-climbs (he developed his skill bringing milk from his farm to Munich in the early 1920s). He won his first race in Baden-Baden in 1923 and then graduated to Austro-Daimlers. He showed so much promise that Ferdinand Porsche built him an Auto Union and he promptly won GPs in Germany, Switzerland and Czechoslovakia. He also won the first of three European Mountain titles.

More GP wins in Italy and Germany followed, and he was unbeatable in hill-climbs before the war. German drivers were banned from competition until 1950 so Stuck took Austrian citizenship and beat Ascari at Monza later that year. He competed in hill-climbs in his 60s and also coached his son, Hans-Joachim, in the intricacies of the Nürburgring.

Above: *Hans Stuck*

Name: Hans STUCK
Nationality: Austrian
Born: 27th December 1900
Died: 9th February 1978
Seasons: 1951-1953
Team/manufacturer(s): BRM, AFM, Ferrari
Race wins: 6
Championship wins: 0

Surtees

Below: *John Surtees in his Ferrari*

John Surtees's father owned a motorcycle shop in South London and was a three-time sidecar champion. Surtees was given his first motorbike at the age of 11 and he soon learned to ride and maintain it. He left school at 16, served as a motorcycle engineer for Vincent and had soon won his first bike race.

He enjoyed an incredible career before he was targeted by several F1 teams, and in only his second race he finished runner-up to Jim Clark. In 1961 he drove a Cooper with little success but the following season in a Lola gave him five points' finishes. He then retired from motorcycle racing to concentrate on Formula One, and he joined Ferrari in 1963. He won at the Nürburgring and came fourth in the championship, but more wins in Germany and Italy and good finishes in Holland, Britain, the US and Mexico gave him the 1964 world championship. He remains the only man to have won world titles on two and four wheels.

In 1965, he moved to the US to compete in the CanAm series but was lucky to survive a bad crash in Canada. He returned to F1 at the Belgian Grand Prix, and drove superbly in heavy rain to one of his finest wins in his last race for Ferrari.

He joined Cooper after two races of the 1966 season but suffered four retirements, although he did win in Mexico. The cars were uncompetitive, however, and he rejoined BRM in 1969. The move yielded little so in 1970, fed up with other people's mechanical inadequacies, Surtees started his own Formula One team.

Team Surtees used V8 Cosworth engines and showed some early promise but the team struggled financially and withdrew from F1 in 1978. Surtees then retired from motorsport and enjoyed a successful career as a property developer. Tragically, his son, Henry, was killed after being struck on the head by a wheel at Brands Hatch in 2009.

Name: John SURTEES, MBE
Nationality: British
Born: 11th February 1934
Seasons: 1960-1972
Team/manufacturer(s): Lotus, Cooper, Lola, Ferrari, Honda, BRM, McLaren, Surtees
Grand Prix: 113
Race wins: 6
Championship wins: 1

Tambay

Patrick Tambay came from a wealthy family and was educated in France and the USA. His racing career began in the early 1970s when he won the Pilote Elf scheme, which led to a successful year in Formula Renault in 1973.

He graduated to European Formula Two and he remained with the series until 1977, after which he was offered a drive by John Surtees. He failed to qualify for the French Grand Prix but scored points later in the season for Theodore. He joined McLaren in 1978 but had little success and it wasn't until he signed for Ferrari midway through the 1982 season that his career took off. He won his fourth race for the team, and won again in San Marino in early 1983, a year in which he finished fourth overall.

He left Ferrari for Renault and then Lola, but could not match his earlier success and retired from F1 at the end of 1986. He raced sportscars at Le Mans,

finishing fourth in 1989, and also ran a sports promotion company.

Above: *Patrick Tambay of France is on two wheels in his Scuderia Ferrari during a race*

Name: Patrick TAMBAY
Nationality: French
Born: 25th June 1949
Seasons: 1977-1979, 1981-1986
Team/manufacturer(s): Surtees, Theodore, McLaren, Ligier, Ferrari, Renault, Lola
Grand Prix: 123
Race wins: 2
Championship wins: 0

Trulli

Below: *Jarno Trulli attends the Toyota Motor Corporation's press briefing*

Jarno Trulli's parents were motorsport fans and he was named after Jarno Saarinen, a Finnish motorcycle champion who was killed at Monza in 1973. A promising career in karting saw him win the Italian and European championships before he moved up to Formula Three.

A win in the 1996 German Championship led to a drive with the Minardi Formula One team the following year. He came fourth in Germany but then moved to Prost for 1998 and 1999, although he struggled with uncompetitive cars.

A switch to Jordan in 2000 yielded four points finishes but several retirements and it wasn't until 2003 with Renault that he made an impact on the championship. His ten points-scoring finishes saw him finish eighth in the drivers' standings. He recorded his first win at Monaco in 2004 and finished sixth overall with 46 points but, after a dispute with the team, he signed for Toyota for the last two races of the season.

Trulli had a solid 2005 and finished seventh in the championship with 43 points, but he couldn't repeat this the following year. Despite showing early promise, Trulli's career with Toyota gradually petered out. He'd finished on the podium three times in his first five races for the Japanese outfit (in 2005) but he could only manage five points-scoring positions in the whole of the next season. 2007 was another difficult year but 2008 and 2009 saw a return to form of sorts and he scored another four podium finishes.

He was always destined for mid-table mediocrity however, and a move to Lotus for 2010 and 2011 yielded no points. Lotus were rechristened Caterham for 2012 and Vitaly Petrov was given Trulli's seat, leaving F1 without an Italian driver for the first time since 1969.

Name: Jarno TRULLI
Nationality: Italian
Born: 13th July 1974
Seasons: 1997-2011
Team/manufacturer(s): Minardi, Prost, Jordan, Renault, Toyota, Lotus
Grand Prix: 256
Race wins: 1
Championship wins: 0

Varzi

Achille Varzi was the son of a prosperous textile manufacturer, and he was a talented motorcycle racer in his youth. He competed at the Isle of Man TT seven times in the 1920s but switched to car racing in 1928 to challenge the great Nuvolari. In Maseratis and Alfa Romeos he won his national championship in 1930 and 1934, and drove to six GP wins in the latter.

He joined Auto Union but only managed four wins in the next three years. His career was then overshadowed by Bernd Rosemeyer and he turned to morphine to cope with the depression. He returned after the war a new man, however, and cemented his comeback with three minor GP wins. During practice for the 1948 Swiss GP, his Alfa flipped and he was crushed to death underneath.

Above: *Achille Varzi at the treacherous 1936 Monaco GP in an Auto Union*

Left: *A serious-looking Varzi*

Name: Achille VARZI
Nationality: Italian
Born: 8th August 1904
Died: 1st July 1948
Seasons: 1924–1948
Team/manufacturer(s): Bugatti, Alfa Romeo, Auto Union, Maserati
Race wins: 18
Championship wins: 0

Vettel

Sebastien Vettel began racing karts at the age of eight, and soon proved himself a talented young driver. By 2003, he had moved on to cars and took the German Formula BMW championship the following year after winning 18 of the 20 races.

In 2005, Vettel joined the Formula Three Euroseries and, by 2007, had made his grand prix debut at the US Grand Prix when filling in for the injured Robert Kubica after the latter's crash in Canada. He impressed immediately, qualifying seventh and finishing in eighth, picking up a well-deserved championship point. At the age of 19 years and 349 days, he broke the record for being the youngest Formula One driver to score a point.

He was then released to join Toro Rosso but endured a difficult start after a crash in Japan. He finished fourth the following week in an underpowered car and raised a few eyebrows. It proved to be a false dawn, however, as Vettel had a dismal start to the 2008 season. But from Monaco onwards he proved himself a champion-in-waiting, notching up a win and several points-scoring finishes.

A move to Red Bull in 2009 finally gave him a car with which he could challenge for the title. He won four races but was pipped to the championship by Jenson Button in a far superior machine. 2010 ushered in a period of total dominance for the young German. He drove brilliantly to score five wins and consistent top-three finishes. The following season he took the title in even more emphatic style, winning 11 races and finishing on the podium at another six. It was a campaign during which he set numerous records.

He didn't have it all his own way in 2012, however. His Red Bull wasn't as consistent and it took a late charge – wins at Singapore, Japan, Korea and India – to seal his third consecutive championship. At the time of writing he is still only 25 and could be the man to beat for a few years yet.

Name: Sebastian VETTEL
Nationality: German
Born: 3rd July 1987
Seasons: 2007-
Team/manufacturer(s): BMW Sauber, Toro Rosso, Red Bull
Grand Prix: 101
Race wins: 26
Championship wins: 3

Villeneuve, Gilles

At the age of nine, Villeneuve's father let him drive the family Volkswagen and a racing legend was born. By the time he was 15 he was repairing an old MGA and often 'borrowed' his dad's Pontiac to cruise the streets.

He eventually managed to get a drive in Formula Ford and was the Quebec Champion in 1973. He then won the Formula Atlantic title in 1976 before being offered a drive with McLaren F1 in 1977. He showed promise in his first season but McLaren decided not to keep him so he signed for Ferrari for the last two races.

By 1982, Villeneuve was regarded as the best driver and was tipped to be the champion, but the season got off to a bad start and he retired in both South Africa and Brazil. Disqualification from the US GP for an illegal rear wing saw him enter the San Marino race weekend with no points. In the race itself, team-mate Didier Pironi disobeyed team orders to slow down and conserve fuel and passed the Canadian on the final lap, depriving Villeneuve of a win. He was incandescent with rage at the betrayal of trust and vowed never to speak to Pironi again.

During qualifying for the Belgian GP at Zolder, Villeneuve's Ferrari clipped the March of Jochen Mass and flew into the air. It then nosedived into an embankment before cartwheeling along the track. Still strapped to his seat, Villeneuve was thrown from the car without his helmet and died in hospital shortly afterwards.

Name: Joseph Gilles Henri VILLENEUVE
Nationality: Canadian
Born: 18th January 1950
Died: 8th May 1982
Seasons: 1977-1982
Team/manufacturer(s): McLaren, Ferrari
Grand Prix: 68
Race wins: 6
Championship wins: 0

Villeneuve, Jacques

Below: *Jacques Villeneuve in 2010*

Jacques Villeneuve was only 11 when his father was killed at Zolder but that didn't stop him following in Gilles's footsteps. He was a promising kart driver and was soon racing Formula Four cars around Imola as a teenager. He then went on a course at the Jim Russell Driving School in Quebec and had graduated to Italian Formula Three by 1989.

He didn't do particularly well so left for Japanese Formula Three in 1992. His driving improved and he ended the season in second place. He then moved to the USA for the Toyota Atlantic series and won five races. In 1994 he was Champ Car Rookie of the Year, and he won the Indy 500 and the championship itself the following season.

Villeneuve's driving came to the attention of Frank Williams and the team principal signed the Canadian for the 1996 season. Villeneuve found himself on pole and eventually finished second in his first race, a race he could have won had he not been asked to let team-mate Damon Hill past. Villeneuve won four races in his first season and ended the season in second overall with 78 points, the best result by a newcomer to the sport. With Hill leaving the team, Villeneuve became Williams's number one in 1997.

His next season was poor because the team had switched from the superb Renault V10 engine to a Mecachrome powerplant, so he moved to BAR in 1999. He struggled with technical problems but remained with the team until 2003, although he only managed two podiums in five years.

Villeneuve was left without a drive in 2004, although he returned at the end of the season with Renault. He then signed a two-year deal with BMW Sauber but he became disillusioned with the sport and walked away mid-2006 to concentrate on racing sportscars.

Name: Jacques Joseph Charles VILLENEUVE
Nationality: Canadian
Born: 9th April 1971
Seasons: 1996-2006
Team/manufacturer(s): Williams, BAR, Renault, Sauber, BMW Sauber
Grand Prix: 165
Race wins: 11
Championship wins: 1

Von Trips

As the son of a noble from the Rhineland, Wolfgang von Trips was a German aristocrat. He began racing after the Second World War and worked his way up to Formula One by the mid-1950s, although he didn't make the start of the 1956 Italian GP.

His first world championship race came the following year in Argentina when he guided his Ferrari to sixth place. He retired at Monaco in his next outing but finished third at Monza in the last race of the season. Although Von Trips came third in France in 1958, he could only finish 11th in the championship.

In 1959, Von Trips drove a Porsche Formula Two car in Monaco but he had a bad crash and was out of action for most of the year. He returned in a Ferrari and drove it to sixth place in the US GP at the end of the season.

Von Trips had a better season in 1960 but he still only scored points at five races and finished a disappointing seventh in the championship. In 1961, however, he was making a determined assault on the title – he

won in Holland and Great Britain and came second in Germany and Belgium – when the teams arrived at Monza. If he finished third or better he would have taken the title but his Ferrari collided with Jim Clark's Lotus before the Parabolica and crashed into a barrier. Von Trips was thrown from the car and killed along with 15 spectators.

Name: Wolfgang Graf Berghe VON TRIPS
Nationality: German
Born: 4th May 1928
Died: 10th September 1961
Seasons: 1956-1961
Team/manufacturer(s): Ferrari, Porsche, Cooper
Grand Prix: 29
Race wins: 2
Championship wins: 0

Above: Wolfgang von Trips getting into his Ferrari before the Italian Grand Prix at Monza. He later crashed into the crowd, killing himself and 15 spectators

Warwick

Right: *Derek Warwick of Great Britain in action in his Lotus Lamborghini*

Derek Warwick started off racing stock cars but graduated to British Formula Three in time to take the 1978 title. He was offered a drive with Toleman three years later but, despite staying with the F1 outfit for three seasons, he enjoyed little success until the back end of the 1983 campaign when he recorded four consecutive points finishes.

A move to Renault in 1984 was supposed to give him a shot at the drivers' crown but the car's reliability let it down and he only managed four podiums. Warwick turned Williams down in 1985 and the seat went instead to Nigel Mansell. Warwick admits this was a mistake as Mansell eventually became world champion with the team. Renault withdrew from Formula One at the end of 1985 and Warwick joined Brabham partway through the 1986 season.

He had little success so signed for Arrows for three years but the cars were uncompetitive so he moved to Lotus and then Footwork, but speed and reliability were still his biggest obstacles. Despite plenty of ability, Warwick never won a race and he retired from F1 at the end of the 1993 season. He drove touring cars for a couple of years before returning to the cockpit for the GP Masters series in 2005.

Name: Derek Stanley Arthur WARWICK
Nationality: British
Born: 27th August 1954
Seasons: 1981-1993
Team/manufacturer(s): Toleman, Renault, Brabham, Arrows, Lotus, Footwork
Grand Prix: 147
Race wins: 0
Championship wins: 0

Watson

Above: *Watson driving a McLaren at the 1982 US GP in Detroit*

John Watson was born in Belfast. He began racing an Austin Healey Sprite in the early 1960s and then had a spell in single-seaters before moving to England to further his career.

He worked his way up to Formula Two and showed enough promise to be given a drive in an old Brabham BT37 at the 1973 British Grand Prix. He retired from the race and suffered the same fate at the US Grand Prix later in the season.

He scored points at three races in 1974 but 1975 was poor by comparison and he joined Penske at the end of the year. He recorded his first win at the 1976 Austrian Grand Prix and two more podiums saw him finish the season seventh overall. Two quiet years with Brabham preceded a move to McLaren, although he had to wait until 1981 for his first win for the team. The 1982 season saw him in contention for the title – he won in Belgium and the USA – but poor reliability in the latter half of the campaign saw his hopes fade and Keke Rosberg took the title.

He also drove well in 1983, with his last win coming at the US GP after he'd started 22nd on the grid. He then retired from Formula One, although he was coaxed out of retirement to race at the 1985 European Grand Prix at Brands Hatch. He went on to race sportscars for a couple of seasons and then founded his own racing school before working as a television commentator.

> **Name:** John Marshall WATSON, MBE
> **Nationality:** British
> **Born:** 4th May 1946
> **Seasons:** 1973-1985
> **Team/manufacturer(s):** Penske, Brabham, McLaren
> **Grand Prix:** 152
> **Race wins:** 5
> **Championship wins:** 0

Webber

Below: *Mark Webber*

The son of an Australian motorcycle dealer, Mark Webber started off in motocross before switching to karts and winning the New South Wales state championship in 1993. He moved to Australian Formula Ford and then came to Europe to further his career in Formula Three. He had a brief spell in sportscar racing but had a spectacular crash at Le Mans in 1999 and returned to Formula 3000.

He impressed enough to be offered a test with Arrows in Barcelona, and he was then signed by Benetton as their reserve driver for 2001. Minardi snapped him up for the 2002 season but, despite a strong showing at his home GP, he struggled for the remainder of the year in an underpowered car. Jaguar took him in 2003 and 2004 and he drove consistently well if not spectacularly but Williams had seen enough to take him in 2005.

He picked up his first podium in Monaco and eventually finished 10th in the championship with 36 points. However, he had less success with Cosworth power in 2006

and managed just seven points throughout the season. Webber signed for Red Bull at the end of the year and it proved to be a watershed moment in his career. Until then he'd finished no higher than 10th in the championship but the upsurge in fortune was gradual, despite a podium finish at the 2007 European Grand Prix. He started 2008 strongly, scoring points at six of the first eight races, but then his season faltered and he retired or finished poorly in the remaining races.

He showed what he was capable of in the next campaign, however, with four podiums, wins in Germany and Brazil, and fourth place in the drivers' standings. The next two seasons he went even closer, narrowly losing out to team-mate Vettel in numerous races and the overall championship. 2012 was a tougher season but he still recorded two wins – in Monaco and Britain – and eventually finished sixth overall with 179 points.

Name: Mark Alan WEBBER
Nationality: Australian
Born: 27th August 1976
Seasons: 2002-
Team/manufacturer(s): Minardi, Jaguar, Williams, Red Bull
Grand Prix: 198
Race wins: 9
Championship wins: 0

Wimille

Jean-Pierre Wimille was a driver of extraordinary skill who would certainly have won the Formula One title had the championship been inaugurated earlier than 1950. He was born in Paris to a motoring enthusiast father and he was soon racing. He made his top-flight debut in a Bugatti at the 1930 French GP, but it would be another two years before he recorded his first win at Lorraine.

In 1934 he signed up as a works driver for the team and promptly won the Algerian GP, and Le Mans twice, the latter victory in 1937 with Pierre Veyron (who lent his name to Bugatti's latest supercar). He won nine GPs in quick succession after the war and would have claimed more but for team orders. He crashed and died at the wheel during practice for the 1949 Argentinean Grand Prix after swerving to avoid a spectator.

Above: *Wimille at the wheel of his Alfa in 1948*

Left: *Jean-Pierre Wimille having won the 1936 Deauville GP*

Name: Jean-Pierre WIMILLE
Nationality: French
Born: 26th February 1908
Died: 28th January 1949
Seasons: 1932-1948
Team/manufacturer(s): Bugatti, Alfa Romeo
Race wins: 20
Championship wins: 0

ALSO AVAILABLE IN THIS SERIES

BRITISH AND IRISH
LIONS
PLAYER BY PLAYER

A COMPILATION OF THE 100 GREATEST BRITISH AND IRISH LIONS PLAYERS

LIAM McCANN

FOREWORD BY TOM SMITH

ALSO AVAILABLE IN THIS SERIES

DARTS
PLAYER BY PLAYER

A COMPILATION OF THE 50 GREATEST DARTS PLAYERS

ANDREW O'BRIEN

ALSO AVAILABLE IN THIS SERIES

THE ASHES
PLAYER BY PLAYER

A COMPILATION OF THE GREATEST PLAYERS TO HAVE PLAYED IN THE ASHES

PAT MORGAN

ALSO AVAILABLE IN THIS SERIES

SNOOKER
PLAYER BY PLAYER

A COMPILATION OF THE 100 GREATEST SNOOKER PLAYERS

LIAM McCANN

The pictures in this book were provided courtesy of the following:

GETTY IMAGES
101 Bayham Street, London NW1 0AG

WIKICOMMONS
commons.wikimedia.org

Design & Artwork by: Scott Giarnese & Alex Young

Published by: Demand Media Limited & G2 Entertainment Limited

Publishers: Jason Fenwick & Jules Gammond

Written by: Liam McCann